in his own words

Peter Gabriel

Mick St. Michael

OMNIBUS PRESS
LONDON · NEW YORK · PARIS · SYDNEY · COPENHAGEN · MADRID

Copyright © 1994 Omnibus Press
(A Division of Book Sales Limited)

Edited by Chris Charlesworth.
Cover & book designed by Michael Bell Design.
Picture research by David Brolan.

ISBN 0.7119.3635.8
Order No. OP47500

Exclusive Distributors:
Book Sales Limited
8/9 Frith Street,
London W1V 5TZ, UK.

Music Sales Corporation
257 Park Avenue South,
New York, NY10010, USA.

Music Sales Pty Limited
30-32 Carrington Street,
Sydney, NSW 2000, Australia.

To the Music Trade only:
Music Sales Limited
8/9, Frith Street,
London W1V 5TZ, UK.

Photo credits: front cover: London Features International; back cover: London Features International,
Armando Gallo/Retna, Famous; Peter Anderson/SIN: 44, 60, 63, 64; Adrian Boot/Retna: 74, 91t;
Bill Davila/Retna: 91b; Famous: back cover b, 50b, 51t&b, 81t&b, 83, 85t&b, 90; Armando Gallo/
Retna: back cover c, 10, 37, 48t&b, 76; Steve Gillett: 50t, 56, 65t&b, 78b; Elliot Landy/Star File: 57;
Bob Leafe/Star File: 38t&b; front cover, back cover t, London Features International: 8, 9, 13, 14, 15,
19, 26, 29, 30, 33, 39, 42t, 45, 52, 55b, 58, 59, 62, 69, 84, 86, 87, 88, 94, 96; Peter Noble/SIN: 66, 67;
Barry Plummer: 12, 16, 17, 20, 21, 22, 23, 24, 25, 27, 34t, 35, 36, 40, 41, 53, 54, 55t, 68, 70, 89;
Neal Preston/Retna: 73; Chuck Pulin/Star File: 11, 32, 42b, 46, 47, 61, 79t&b; Paul Rider/
Retna: 78t; Mick Rock/Star File: 4, 6; Vinnie Zuffante/Star File: 72, 92.

Every effort has been made to trace the copyright holders of the photographs in this book but one or
two were unreachable. We would be grateful if the photographers concerned would contact us.

A catalogue record for this book is available from the British Library.

Thanks to Richard Carman.

Printed in the United Kingdom by Scotprint Limited, Musselburgh, Edinburgh.

Introduction

Although he's currently close to completing his second decade
as a solo artist, Peter Gabriel will inevitably be remembered by
any thirty-something rock fan as the frontman of Genesis in their
most exciting and groundbreaking period from 1967 to 1974.
His split from them signalled the start of not one but three musical
success stories: his own solo career, the continuing (and, it must
be said, even more lucrative) Genesis saga, plus the emergence
of his successor, Phil Collins, as the world's most popular
singing drummer.

This book concerns itself with Gabriel's utterances both pre- and
post-Genesis, his thoughts on rejoining them for a single concert
in 1984 to bail out the ailing WOMAD world music organisation
in which he'd invested much time and effort, and of course his
own solo work. This includes albums of songs, film soundtracks,
and award-winning videos. He now has his own label and studio,
both sharing the name Real World, is continuing to champion
Third World music and is second only to Paul Simon in bringing
the music of non-traditional rock countries to the West's attention.

In his private life, Gabriel's restless heart seems to bring both
pain and pleasure. He has survived a stormy, on-off marriage and
a series of subsequent high-profile relationships. Actress Rosanna
Arquette, singer Sinéad O'Connor and supermodel Claudia
Schiffer are among the eligible ladies the tabloid press has bracketed
with his name. Yet despite the playboy tag they may try to foist
on him, Gabriel's genuine concerns have led him to tour to
promote Amnesty International and act as their unpaid spokesman.
In the midst of all this, his personal fortune has climbed back from
the brink to the point where the financial press reported his 1992
earnings as a cool £1.6 million.

Peter Gabriel is certainly no 'here today, gone tomorrow' pop
star. During a quarter of a century in the recording business he has
expressed opinions on many different subjects, most of which are
as engrossing as his music. This book can represent only a carefully
selected sample of those thoughts, but it may give his many fans
some invaluable background as to the workings of an exceedingly
complex character.

Early Days

Growing Up

"My mother is from a musical family… her mother used to sing with Sir Henry Wood at the Promenade Concerts, and her various sisters had been to the Royal Academy, so I started to learn piano because everybody in her family did. But I was having so many lessons… so when I was nine I had a little revolution and said, 'No more piano lessons, no more riding lessons, I'm going to stop all this and watch TV'. So I stopped it, and they said, 'You'll regret it when you're older', and I did regret it when I was older."

"My father was born into a family of timber merchants – Gabriel, Wade and English. Most of the family members – particularly the duds – had safe jobs with the family firm. My father was much more of a thinker than the rest of them and more inclined towards scientific things. He studied at the University of London and became an electrical engineer. He was involved with the development of radar flight simulators and he designed a cable TV system called Dial-A-Programme, which was, I believe, the first operating TV system using fibre optics."

"I had a very happy and free childhood. My father was an influence in the sense that he was always in his workshop and he used to build things out of nothing. He has a very creative mind. And my mother's piano playing was regularly sinking into my subconscious."

"My childhood was spent playing with animals and lots of little girls. I had a very liberated sex life, between the ages of 4 and 7, which I never really recovered from.

"That provided much open and liberated and safe sex. I think it was my first experience of sadism because there was one girl who used to love using stinging nettles in strange ways. I'll leave the rest to your imagination."

"There were times when I would be left to my own devices. My mother and sister were both into riding and pony clubs. This didn't appeal to me so I would find myself wandering around in a world of my own. That's probably when I started my preoccupation with fantasy."

"It seemed claustrophobic to me in some ways. There was an enormous amount of love and, latterly, an enormous amount of support, but it wasn't always as open as I wanted it to be."

"My mother's family were all musical, a very Victorian family with five sisters, all of whom would play different instruments and sing together on musical evenings. I used to hate it as a teenager but, I think, some of it must have sunk in. Around Christmas time, there always used to be a collection of aunts gathering around the grand piano."

"I think I found it quite easy to get on with other kids. I wasn't a macho, sporty male. I would prefer doctors and nurses with the girls behind the flower beds to cowboys and indians."

"I went to nursery school about 200 yards down the road, then there was a prep school which was in the other direction, towards Woking. That was where most of the flowerbed activities took place. And then, just a little further down the hill was St Andrews School for boys. I boarded there for my last year, which was a relatively peaceful transition for me as I could cycle home for weekends."

Charterhouse

"I hated it. It was terrible. I think I was very sensitive at school, everything was a huge great drama, and many nights I would spend awake trying to get to sleep."

"Going to Charterhouse was traumatic. I remember the first night. There were no curtains in the dormitory and it was very bleak and cold. I'd been used to living in the country; even the prep school had been very quiet at night-time.

   "It was a real wrench feeling that I'd been thrown into this cold, merciless environment. And, at the time, Charterhouse still had remnants of *Tom Brown's School Days*. There were monitors beating fags and a lot of structured cruelty within the system. It was very definitely a shock."

"You'd arrive and there would be this huge room with little dormitories divided by hardboard, and you'd hear all these strange voices late at night. It was dark and by a road, so it felt to me like the films of the First World War I had seen: ack-ack guns and big flares lighting up the sky, as the car headlights went by on the road outside. And everyone seemed to be nervous and unhappy, and there were some boys crying when I first went there."

"There used to be boys from the nearby state schools who would hide in the gorse bushes and beat us up and take our bicycles. So we ended up forming a gang, as a means of self-defence. We'd gradually gather, and by the time we got within a mile of the school, there were about fifteen boys, all cycling together. This meant that there was a good chance you could outnumber the opposition! I hate the class system, and I think that the school system is one of the most effective means by which this country perpetuates its class divisions."

"All through the first year I felt miserable. There was this
incredible power set-up, you know, with the older boys having
fags – the younger boys – to do all their menial duties, clean their
shoes, and so on. It was really crazy. I think I was very sensitive
at school, everything was a great drama, and many nights I
would spend awake trying to get to sleep. The senior boys in
the dormitory were allowed to talk, and they would talk about
anything, and try to impress the other boys. Cars, girlfriends…
all sorts of cocky sensationalism."

"You were taught to be leaders of men. You had the feeling that
you were being trained as a race apart. You were not encouraged
to mix with the boys in the town. All sorts of shocking, ideological
stuff was just pumped into you.

"I suppose it gave us, as insecure teenagers, some kind of
foothold with which to take on 'life' – at that age you aren't about
to question things that are giving you some sort of support.

"I remember the billiard room vividly; it was the only place
that we could play music. It had this really beaten up, old Dansette
record player in a wooden cabinet. You could only play it for
about an hour and a half every day. I used to take my Otis
Redding records in there and turn them up full volume and dance
until I was in a frenzied sweat. This ritual gave me an immense
feeling of relief."

"I remember that Tony (Banks) and I were both lectured about
mixing with 'undesirable elements' as our housemaster called them.
This included 'Rutherford', but not Ant (Anthony Phillips).
Ant was very good at cricket, and our housemaster was a real
cricket fan. Even though Ant did have these slight tendencies for
disreputable behaviour, all was recovered on the cricket pitch."

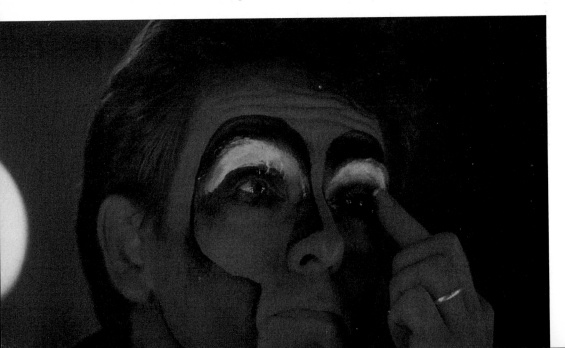

Dressing Up

"From about fifteen onwards, I began to get a sense of idealism from reading things that introduced me to new points of view. Then, towards the end of my time at school, came the flower-power era and all the great breakthroughs that came with it – The Beatles, drugs, long hair. It was all tremendously exciting to observe this Colditz in the middle of suburbia. And occasionally I would sneak away and go to clubs like Middle Earth in London."

"There was this whole exciting world of hippies and Carnaby Street and *Rave* magazine that I could only be part of during the school holidays. There was no way that our music was touching any of this. Clothes seemed to offer a way in."

"I found this old hat in my grandfather's dressing-up box. I took it round all sorts of different shops in London to see if I could find a hat manufacturer, and ended up at Dunn and Co in Piccadilly. I don't know what they must have thought when they saw this spotty-looking schoolboy walking in with this strange hat. I think the old guy, who was running the place, was quite amused by it. They took it in and had a look at it and sent it round to their factory, where they said that they could make them.

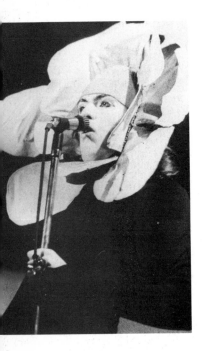

"I wanted bright colours so they had them done in pinks and purples and yellows and greens and oranges – all sorts of very loud, gaudy colours. And then, I had to take them round boutiques to try and flog them. One of the most exciting moments of my childhood was coming home from school, and switching on *Juke Box Jury* to see Marianne Faithfull wearing one of my hats. I nearly wet myself!

"I also used to try and increase my pocket money at school by dyeing people's shirts for 10p a go, and this got me into a certain amount of trouble because they went into the wash with the cricket whites, which then came out pink or green! So that came to a halt.

"There was this very naïve fantasy going round at the time that a revolution, a sudden surge of idealism, was going to come through the music and the clothes – indeed, through youth."

Early Musical Efforts

"I was all right until I went to Charterhouse. Then I got fat and spotty. I used to think that I didn't have what it took to get the girls, so I became a rock musician like The Beatles and The Rolling Stones, because they never seemed to have any trouble getting the girls. No, it wasn't quite that simple… I wanted the money too!

"I started off trying to write songs at about eleven or twelve. The first song I wrote was called 'Sammy The Slug'. Everyone else was writing about girls, and I was writing about slugs, which shows what I was interested in!

"I had this dream when I was eleven, and I saw a fork in the path where I could either be an entertainer or singer, or farmer. I used to dream very vividly then. Not so much now. Now I get daydreams when I'm half awake, but the night time stuff I don't remember so much. But I never thought that I would be a singer, because I didn't think that I could sing. When I was young they thought that I had a nice choirboy voice, but when I tried to sing rock songs it sounded terrible."

"I liked to play drums, because I thought, 'Well, this is where it's all at, where it comes from – rhythm', and I was given a snare drum by my parents when I was thirteen. Then this friend Andrew Ramage's brother had an old Premier tom-tom which he sold to me for seven pounds and ten shillings. He told me it was a bad drum, but I was determined to get it because it was a real drum. It was like the ones they used in *Six Five Special* on TV, and I thought, 'This is great, it doesn't matter what it sounds like, it'll make a noise when I hit it, I can hit it hard.'"

"I used to play drums in a dance band called M'Lords and then in a soul band called The Spoken Word. I wanted to be a drummer at that point, but at the same time, I realised that I also wanted to write songs."

"It was very bad. It was funny because I was definitely right at
the back. The drummer of the dance band was a very unspectacular
character."

"My parents were disappointed that I didn't go to university.
And then that I didn't go to film school, which I rejected so I
could work with Genesis. Their prime concern was not really that
my lifestyle was rebellious – although we had traditional arguments
about length of hair and so forth – but that I wouldn't be able to
get a job later on and make a living." (1986)

The Genesis of Genesis

Stepping Out

"Playing in the band was more Mike and Ant's thing at the time. I was just an afterthought, I think. Tony was originally going to play the keyboards, and then he used that as a wedge to get one or two of our songs onto a tape that was done in Chiswick at a friend called Brian Roberts' studio.

"Richard McPhail, who later became our tour manager, was really the main singer, and he was a better singer and performer than I was at the time. But then the others seemed to prefer my voice to Richard's. Or maybe Tony just wheedled me in; I can't remember."

"My first compositions tended to be over complex because I was trying to do everything that everyone else hadn't done. Then we started to do things together and while we were still at school, we actually wrote one or two songs, which appeared on 'From Genesis To Revelation'."

"I think Tony and I were beginning to build up a rapport of sorts. There were definitely things about each other's early musical offerings that we didn't like. But there were many elements that we did like and so we concentrated on them. I think that it was when we started to write songs together, that we thought we might get them recorded."

"Tony and I were thinking of being songwriters, whereas Mike and Ant were really into playing in a group and doing Stones imitations at parties... I also wanted to play the drums, but not so much with this kind of material."

Genesis in 1973.

"I had definitely got into beat music and soul music in my first few years at Charterhouse. I think it was a sort of express train into the heart. These people were singing as if they meant it. Most of the shit one heard on the radio had no real feeling behind it, like so much pop music. With soul singers there's a really powerful emotion there – whether they mean the words or not."

"There was undoubtedly an old boy network. I think as Phil and Steve did not come from public school, they thought that the three of us had it all tied up."

"This is what really interests me when I see other bands – their internal structure. It's interesting to observe any group of people that are functioning as a collaborative team on a creative project as there's always an immense amount of ego manipulation.

"There were moments socially when we still had a lot of fun. But, once we got down to the serious business... phew! I think it forced people to come up with some really good stuff, because they knew if it didn't work, it was going to get shot down. You were at risk of being slaughtered. I think the only person who managed to get away with things not everyone liked was Tony! I was machiavellian and manipulative about trying to get my way."

"We had some material that was not given a chance because we were inept at recognising its strong points and making those work. I feel that Genesis could have broken through to much bigger audiences had we found ourselves a charismatic producer, rather than using a sort of laid-back engineer-type producer.

"I really felt that, if we could find the right charismatic producer with a strong enough personality and a good sense of music, that they could, as an outsider, help us make the right decisions regarding the material. I couldn't do it as I was obviously prejudiced. I had my bits, and if I said that I didn't think someone else's bit worked, then they would say that a bit of mine didn't work. Ridiculous, petty band politics.

"It was a pretty unattractive role for anyone to take on as it would have meant really upsetting people as well as getting upset yourself. It was almost like a religion – through our muddled, neurotic, paranoid processes, we'd arrived at this thing which was called music, and to challenge it, at that point, was like questioning someone's religious beliefs. And yet, we needed it; I longed for that person to come along."

"We used to go to Decca, give our name at the desk, and the man would phone up and say 'There's a group called The Janitors here to see you'. Towards the end of our relationship with the label, I think they began to catch on to the way that newer progressive labels like Charisma and Island were scooping up the talent and the sales, because we got a letter saying 'We now have an artist relations manager – come along and chat to him whenever you want'. By then, it was too late."

"Throughout the group's career, I think, I was the one doing the hustling and trying to link them up to the real world. It was always a sort of gamble, and my grandfather on my mother's side was a considerable gambler. I've always liked the feeling that there is a risk element – that something around me may go well or badly.

"The trouble with hustling was that I wasn't very good at it. I would go in, as I see many people do today and get palmed off by the telephonist, or receptionist. You end up spending the whole day there, and you don't get to see anyone.

"Occasionally, one of the others would come with me to give me moral support, but they usually had better things to do. They didn't seem to take it that seriously. I thought this was dumb because, if we didn't get a deal, nothing was going to happen. They used to think that they could just go on making music in the cottage."

"I remember quite clearly the time I approached Warner Brothers. I found out the Christian name of the Managing Director and walked right in and said, 'Is Ian back from lunch?' The receptionist said, 'No.' To which I replied, 'OK, I'll just go and wait in his office then'. She was nervous because it sounded like I was a personal friend of the MD. This way I got right into the inner sanctum, and was able to hand over the sweaty little tape. Not that it did any good but at least the rejection came from the top."

"I remember Tony and I going to see one agency, and the guy sat us down in his office. He listened to the music and then, very deliberately, told us that we should go back to whatever we'd been doing before, giving us some good reasons why. I felt as if a black cloud which had been hovering in the distance had actually come down and engulfed us. It was most unpleasant. The worst of it was that we'd go straight back to the rehearsal room to play this music – this magic that we were convinced could inspire the world!"

"There was another guy called Alec, who did a tape with us at Ant's house. This tape then got into the hands of Paul Samwell-Smith who was then producing Cat Stevens and was the hot producer of the time. He agreed to go into the BBC studios with us at Shepherd's Bush, and do a demo of some music which was going to be for a TV programme. I think it was for an *Arena* programme about a painter, a classic futuristic film of the Thirties called *Alphaville*.

"Samwell-Smith did the demos with us, and that was the first time that I ever thought Genesis sounded good. The others were very suspicious of Samwell-Smith because of the rendering power to someone else. I was certain that he was making us sound better than we could do on our own."

The Jonathan King Connection

"Jonathan King told us we would be on *Top Of The Pops* so we all went out and bought new clothes. The idea was that they would all be either black or white… I wanted us to be different from all the other stuff coming out of Carnaby Street, because it was all very bright colours."

"We were using the old boy network. And I think, at that time, King seemed quite happy to use the young boy network. He gave us some money to experiment with and told us to produce a demo.

"He was interested, and I would have to go down to the phone box out of school on the hill, and struggle with my coins and the pip box, to try and locate this person from the pop business. At that point, everyone who was involved with the music business was regarded with suspicion, including King."

"We talked about a name for the group with King. His first suggestion, which the rest of the band have forgotten although I haven't, was Gabriel's Angels – which didn't seem to register with the others.

"King actually suggested it again when we found there was another band called Genesis in America, and we were considering a name change. I think his thinking was that some of the stuff was influenced by hymns, and so this new name suggested an absurd, naïve innocence."

"All the original demos that King had heard were with acoustic instruments, which he thought gave us quite a novel sound. He's shrewd – King – and much better at spotting hits than making them and he came up with quite a lot of outrageous ideas for us. He was an interesting person to be dealing with."

Peter on stage with Dave Jackson of Van Der Graaf Generator.

Formative Influences

"Tony and I used to go down to Record Corner in Godalming… we would hang around there and listen to soul records, people like Otis Redding and James Brown. We'd sneak there very bravely, because loafing around in cafés and record shops of the town was out and if we were caught we would have been punished."

"The first album I had was The Beatles' first album. I can remember exactly where I was when I first heard 'Love Me Do'. There are probably ten records where I can recall the emotional excitement and hearing something which was new, earthy and gutsy. Like Nina Simone's 'I Put A Spell On You' for example.
   "I remember when they made the first world-wide TV satellite link, with The Beatles singing 'All You Need Is Love'. It felt like, 'We've made it'. Very naïve stuff, but I was very excited. I felt part of the generation. It was a really exciting thing to watch and feel – even if you were just a spectator, which I was. I was just a weekend hippy."

"The first gig that I went to was John Mayall's Bluesbreakers at The Marquee." (1992)

"The way (Otis Redding) could generate feeling and excitement, that was an up-tempo memory for me. But the strong, soulful, passionate ballads were also amazing.
   "There was an energy there which I think you don't see elsewhere. Springsteen gets close at times, but it's a little more thought out. I think with Otis it was direct from the gut. He was my hero as a singer, definitely, and a lot of that music was part of what drove me to consider music for myself. I was a teenager, very impressionable and very ready to be impressed."

Phil Collins Then...

"There was a definite change when Phil came into the band.
He was a real drummer – something I was never that convinced
of with Chris Stewart or John Mayhew. Up until then, we were
a group of fairly ramshackle musicians, trying hard to communicate
through our music. Most of our ideas were in the form of songs
and riffs and melodies – playing our instruments was somewhat
secondary."

"Phil was not really a writer at that point, but a musician, and a
very good and professional one. He changed our attitude and
brought us closer together as a band."

Phil Collins.

"Phil actually knew musicians, which was something that
the rest of us didn't. We'd come across a few on the road and got
friendly with some that we toured with, but were never part of
a circuit of musicians who went to clubs and did sessions."

"I remember the first phone call I had with Phil – he told me that
he'd played on a George Harrison session, which impressed me a
lot. He was actually second tambourine, I think, but he had played
alongside one of The Beatles – that was big time!"

"Phil was always very approachable, he also knew a lot of people.
He could actually touch people; he would put his arm around
someone's shoulder when he was talking. This is something I
can do nowadays, but, at that time, it was a big problem. I was
more of a neurotic, middle-class, English, socialising-at-a-distance
type person."

"Phil was the critical element in terms of the feel of the music and
I was the critical element in terms of style and presentation."

"Phil could be a terrible coward. I had originally asserted a lot of
influence over the choice of a new drummer and, at the time, I had
felt that I'd got a sort of soul brother in the band, in terms of feel.
    "When there were arguments, I would look to Phil, as I thought
that he would support what I was saying, and he would sit on the
fence, and refuse to budge. Other times, when he was basically
in support of Tony's position and opposed to me, he would still
be afraid of committing himself."

"I felt easy with Phil. There were times at some gigs when we
used to go into a room to get away from it all and sit down
together at a piano. My piano playing was humble, and, at that
point, Phil's was even more humble.
    "We used to sing with each other and get into grooves.
He was very much into an American style of singing, a soft Richie
Havens – the type of singing that you can still hear in some of his
songs today, my style was quite different, a sort of weird English
thing – the way I sounded on 'Willow Farm' in the middle of
'Supper's Ready', or 'Harold The Barrel' or whatever. They were
great moments. I think we would both fantasise then about making
music on our own, or doing things together."

... And Now

"I respect Phil's music and I would like my own to reach as large
an audience as possible, but I would strongly refute the suggestion
that I'm trying to copy him. That pisses me off, because about the
time of my third album there were considerable stylistic changes in
Phil's music and I feel that my influence on him hasn't been fairly
acknowledged." (1986)

Mike Rutherford.

"He's an amazing drummer. I'd forgotten quite how good he is.
It was interesting to see what he came up with for my songs.
I think he had a good time just drumming and not having to sing
at all." (1979)

"I've steered more of a middle course (than Phil). The thing I still
like best is to hear him playing the drums." (1993)

Tony Banks

"Tony was a bit edgy. I felt I had a hard time socialising but I
think he had an even harder time. I think that really, my friendship
with Tony developed out of a mutual interest in the piano. As
soon as the games period finished we would have a fight for access
to the piano. Sometimes this would mean clambering through the
food hatch in order to beat the person running through the door.
It was that critical."

"Tony was always the most difficult about having his stuff rejected.
We'd all submit bits, and people would only like a certain number
of them. After he'd stormed out of the room twice, you didn't
want another major explosion from him, so you'd say, 'OK, Tony,
let's go with that'.
    "Then Phil would have to work very hard to try and loosen up
Tony's stuff. Mike's stuff tended – and my stuff too, I think – to
have more feel to it. But Tony used to come up with some great
melodies."

"Tony and I knew each other very well by now, and we were
a combination of best friends and worst enemies. Like any long-
term relationship, as with a married couple for instance, you get
to know each other's Achilles' heel. You turn the screw and you
know exactly how to pulverise the opposition. He was slightly
better at it than me, largely because he had a better defence
mechanism. It was all part and parcel of our relationship, which
included moments that were really positive and good."

Mike Rutherford

"I felt that Mike and I could talk things through and change positions or at least admit to being seen to change positions. Tony was more insecure in some ways, and could not be seen to let go of what he'd originally argued for."

Steve Hackett

"Tony and I went to this little flat in Ebury Bridge Road that belonged to Steve's parents. He and his brother, John, had this tiny room. They started playing the tape, and there was some slight King Crimson influences. There were also some acoustic things with a slightly Spanish flavour, which were very idiosyncratic."

"Steve began to assert himself before Phil, and insisted on getting some songs through. There were some things that we all liked but there was also quite a lot that we didn't. I think that was partly because Steve was less able to manipulate the rest of us then as we were."

What They Say About Him

"Basically, it was Mike and Ant recording their songs, and I was asked along to play keyboards. Peter arrived on the second day and we persuaded Ant, who had been doing the vocals (which were really terrible!), that Pete had the better voice – so after that he did the singing." (Tony Banks)

"Peter was into all sorts of things. Peter was a clever boy. He had some hats made by Dunns. Have you ever heard about Peter's hats? Everyone used to buy his hats. He also used to dye everybody's T-shirts for them at Charterhouse. Our white shirts became turquoise. A colourful man, Peter. He always had a lot of creative ideas." (Ant Phillips)

"Peter is what you might call rather vague. He has always been like that and that's how he was when he rang up and said 'Um, ah, well, we'd, er, like, um, well, if you'd like to come down and sort of play with us and um…'. That's how he is – positive, but vague." (Phil Collins)

"Pete and I were friends and we used to work things out together. He used to have the sheet music for various pieces that I'd never actually heard of and I quite enjoyed playing along with him. We were close friends the whole time we were at school together but it wasn't until people like Otis Redding that we found that we really liked the same kind of music. 'I Put A Spell On You' was another song that we both like a lot." (Tony Banks)

"He said, 'It's Peter Gabriel here. I've seen your advert and we've got a band together, but the guitarist has left, and we've got another guy but he's not working out. If you want to see us we're doing a free Christmas show at the Lyceum.

"They had a standing ovation and although it was a free gig, the crowd was really behind the band. I thought I could at least do as well as the guitarist they were employing. I went to Peter when he was on the side and had a few words with him. He was very nervous and looking around and stuff." (Steve Hackett)

"When I joined the band, I thought, 'Well Pete's obviously the instigator – he's the man who's always on the telephone; he's the main hustler'. At the same time I felt that he often found it difficult to explain himself. We used to have surreal conversations, where neither of us really understood what the other was saying." (Steve Hackett)

And then there were three... Phil Collins, Mike Rutherford and Tony Banks.

The Split with Genesis

The Prelude

"Genesis was a collaborative venture – a co-operative – all the royalties were being split equally, and there was quite a lot of idealism. And then, suddenly, I was being singled out as the front man, the performer. I was doing the interviews. People assumed that I did all the writing.

"In order to try and redress the balance, I played down my role. When people said they wrote songs, what they often meant was that they wrote the chord sequences. Again, if the melodies and the lyrics were put down afterwards by me or someone else, that would not be construed as part of the songwriting."

"I used to swallow a lot of that because it was clearly pointed out to me that I was getting an unfair share of the credit from the outside world. All that was reversed after I left, and the band still managed to make music that satisfied all the fans. As a result, people probably assumed that I hadn't written any of the music!"

"I think I had the benefit of the excitement of being the front man. But the penalty for that was that, within the band, there was a hotbed of resentment towards me, which was never openly declared.

"As a result, I was not treated very sympathetically. In other words, they were less prepared to give me space to do things, as they felt that I'd already got more space than I deserved."

Rutherford, Banks and Collins.

"There were a lot of things… it was as much inside the group as it was outside the group."

"Around the time we started work on 'The Lamb' I had this call from Hollywood from William Friedkin who'd seen the story I'd written on the back of the live album and he thought it indicated a weird, visual mind. He was trying to put together a sci-fi film and he wanted to get a writer who'd never been involved with Hollywood before.
   "We were working at Headley Grange which I felt was partly haunted by Jimmy Page's black magic experiments, and was full of rock and roll legend. I would go bicycle to the phone box down the hill and dial Friedkin in California with pockets stuffed full of 10p pieces."

"I was pretty good at manipulating but I think by 'The Lamb' the resentment towards me was so big that I had very little space. And I felt the only way I could work was to go into a corner and function on my own. A lot of the melodies were written after the event – after the backing tracks had been put down."

"The pressure was accumulating. I was saying to myself, 'OK, we get successful in America. We get rich. What then? Do we become like the other bands who've made it?'
   "There were things about those groups that I didn't like, and I didn't want to become part of a supergroup. I was beginning to dislike myself for doing what I was doing. I had no idea what I wanted to do, but I knew I was sick of rock, the business, and everything about it. I just wanted to get out."

"I was asked to tour Europe. And do more tours. I felt guilty because I was allegedly destroying Genesis. At least, if we toured Europe, we could pay off most of our debts. Which wasn't the case – we were still in the red when I left."

The Split

"I went into Tony Smith's room and told him I was leaving and he tried to talk me out of it, saying, 'Hold on a couple of days'. I said that I'd been thinking about it a lot and that it was final.
   "The rest of the band were told a few days later in Canada. Their position was that we had worked eight years to get this far, and now, finally, we were about to make it and I was pulling the carpet out from underneath it all.
   "I felt terrible, but I knew that I'd made up my mind, and I can be really obstinate. I wanted a career where I had the opportunity to take on other projects but the band had this army-like attitude. There was no room to be flexible – if you were in the band, you were in it 100 percent, or you were out."

"I had a big lump in my throat when we did the last gigs in France. A big chapter in my life was coming to an end, and I couldn't tell anyone. We had a policy of doing no interviews throughout that tour, but quite often people said, 'We'll only give you space if we can talk to Peter'. Which didn't help matters at all.

"I felt a real sham – I couldn't tell people what was going on. But I'd made an agreement, because I felt so guilty, that I would keep quiet about it until the band had time to sort themselves out."

PG's Own Statement

I HAD A DREAM

"I had a dream, eye's dream. Then I had another dream with the body and soul of a rock star. When it didn't feel good I packed it in. Looking back for the musical and non-musical reasons, this is what I came up with:
OUT. ANGELS OUT – an investigation.

"The vehicle we had built as a co-op to serve our song writing, became our master and had cooped us up inside the success we had wanted. It affected the attitudes and the spirit of the whole band. The music had not dried up and I still respect the other musicians, but our roles had set in hard. To get an idea through 'Genesis the Big' meant shifting a lot more concrete than before. For any band, transferring the heart from idealistic enthusiasm to professionalism is a difficult operation.

"I believe the use of sound and visual images can be developed to do much more than we have done. But on a large scale it needs one clear and coherent direction, which our pseudo-democratic committee system could not provide.

"As an artist, I need to absorb a wide variety of experiences. It is difficult to respond to intuition and impulse within the long term planning that the band needed. I felt I should look at/learn about/develop myself, my creative bits and pieces and pick up on a lot of work going on outside music. Even the hidden delights of vegetable growing and community living are beginning to reveal their secrets. I could not expect the band to tie in their schedules with my bondage to cabbages. The increase in money and power, if I had stayed, would have anchored me to the spotlights. It was important to me to give space to my family which I wanted to hold together, and to liberate the daddy in me.

"Although I have seen and learnt a great deal in the last seven years, I found I had begun to look at things as the famous Gabriel, despite hiding my occupation whenever possible, hitching lifts, etc... I had begun to think in business terms; very useful for an often bitten once shy musician, but treating records and audiences as money was taking me away from them. When performing, there were less shivers up and down the spine.

Genesis in Central Park, New York.

"I believe the world has soon to go through a difficult period of changes. I'm excited by some of the areas coming through to the surface which seem to have been hidden away in people's minds. I want to explore and be prepared, to be open and flexible enough to respond, not tied in to the old hierarchy.

"Much of my psyche's ambitions as 'Gabriel archetypal rock star' have been fulfilled – a lot of the ego-gratification and the need to attract young ladies, perhaps the result of frequent rejection as 'Gabriel acne-struck public-school boy'. However, I can still get off playing the star game once in a while.

"My future within music, if it exists, will be in as many situations as possible. It's good to see a growing number of artists breaking down the pigeon-holes. This is the difference between the profitable, compartmentalized, battery chicken and the free-range. Why did the chicken cross the road anyway?

"There is no animosity between myself and the band or management. The decision had been made some time ago and we have talked about our new directions. The reasons why my leaving was not announced earlier was because I had been asked to delay until they had found a replacement to plug up the hole. It is not impossible that some of them might work with me on other projects.

"I do not express myself adequately in interviews and I felt I owed it to the people who have put a lot of love and energy supporting the band to give an accurate picture of my reasons."

The Aftermath

"They were definitely nervous about carrying on without me. Yet they have proved they could because the band has become a lot bigger than when I was in it. In reality, they shouldn't have been worried. I think I had more confidence in their ability to manage without me than they did because I knew that in the long run, songwriting was what really mattered. And they are good songwriters."

"I saw Genesis again at the Hammersmith Odeon on the next tour. I felt much more at ease than I had expected to, except that I got some twitches in 'Supper's Ready'; it looked like somebody else dressed up in my entrails."

"Now I can watch Phil sing without feeling emotionally attached to a song. I always enjoy watching the interaction between him and Chester on drums."

"There was always a problem about people not coming clean with who was best at doing what. We were not able to own up to it. If we had been able to do that, and had been mature enough to avoid these petty squabbles, the band would have worked a lot better. After I left, and later when Steve had left, there was a period when people could relax. There was one less person to argue with, and because there was less fighting, the production end of it could run much more smoothly.
  "I think one of the major changes which began to happen towards the end of the time I was there, and which has definitely happened since, is that the band learnt how to make the best of the material through production, arrangement and performance."

The 1984 Reunion

"At that point I was so freaked out I would have done anything. I was very touched that they were prepared to do it, to bail me out. Because although I didn't feel personally liable, I had been part of a team that was naïve. A lot of the decisions which were partly responsible for the problems I didn't feel I had created. Except that I had instigated a thing and left it to the WOMADers. I felt responsible in neglecting to take a heavy-handed financial role. I think I would have made some attempts afterwards to pay off what could have been paid. But I wouldn't have been able to get that sort of audience."

"I had been trying for years to get out of these associations, and here I was jumping back into it."

"It was just like returning to some sort of family reunion. It felt really warm, though it was terrible weather. Musically it wasn't very good, but emotionally it was very strong. I was given at Strat's* funeral his notebook in which he wrote some notes at that concert, and he was obviously touched."

*Strat – Tony Stratton-Smith, founder and head of Charisma Records.

The Records

Genesis Albums & Singles

From Genesis To Revelation (album, 1969)

"It was terribly pretentious… the history of Man's evolution in 10 simple pop songs."

"The main thing we were trying to do at that time was break the barrier between folk and rock." (1990)

"'From Genesis To Revelation' was supposed to be the history of the universe, altogether very duff concept. Listening to it now – I think there are some things that showed we had melody-writing potential. That's about all I can say. I think Ant was the best songwriter of us all at that point. Tony did some good melodies, but they were a bit stiff."

"We recorded 'From Genesis To Revelation' in a day, and by the time I got to 'In The Wilderness' which was the most demanding vocal performance, it was pitched above my range. You could hear this desperate sort of retching noise as I struggled for the high notes. I had to keep taking showers, anything to try and keep me awake."

Silent Sun (single)

"I do remember that we tried to write something that sounded like a Bee Gees ballad. I tried to sing a little bit like Robin Gibb on the second verse of 'Silent Sun'. I'm sure we would have denied it at the time, as we have denied other influences at later stages. Anyway it worked and it was put out as a single."

Trespass (album, 1970)

Stagnation (album track)
"Ant and I used to enjoy playing with the words. We would write poems which had nothing to do with songs. He was into flowery, romantic visions, whereas I was into the darker and altogether more mysterious side of life.

"When I look back, it really makes me cringe, but I guess it was all part of growing up. I think 'Stagnation' is one of the numbers which I still regard as archetypal early Genesis. It was one of our more original numbers."

The Knife (album track)
"Tony and I used to go up to the Marquee to see The Nice, who,

unlike ELP, were very concise and, I'd say unpretentious as well
as extremely powerful. Around that period, there was Hendrix,
Vanilla Fudge, The Nice, but not too many others that were both
musical and powerful. I remember sitting down at the piano
trying to write something that had the excitement of 'Rondo'
by The Nice. I played the first riff to Tony, and he was obviously
into it because they were a band that we both liked. After that,
Tony did the second section and then we played 'The Knife'
together."

"We would start with soft numbers and work up to aggressive
ones. If we kept the power in the back, we could introduce
ourselves slowly like a folk band... and then gradually we could
introduce more and more electric instruments and then we would
finish off with 'The Knife', this aggressive number about this
revolutionary figure on a power trip. I knew we had the power
and the balls to grab an audience, and that if we hadn't got them
by then, we would move them one way or another."

"The lyrics for 'The Knife' were partly me being a public
schoolboy rebelling against my background. I'd been heavily
influenced by a book on Gandhi at school, and I think that was
part of the reason I became a vegetarian as well as coming to
believe in non-violence, as a form of protest. And I wanted to
try and show how violent revolutions inevitably end up with
a dictator figure in power."

Nursery Cryme (album, 1971)

The Musical Box (album track)
"My grandfather's house at Cox Hill which later became my
ashram, was the inspiration for 'Musical Box'. There was a formal
garden there with a croquet lawn, goldfish pond, rose garden,
squash court and a greenhouse, surrounded by vines and fig trees.
There was also a shed where my grandfather kept various bits of
exercising equipment. Inside this shed was a wooden railway track,
which was a fantastic toy. It was probably very small, but I
remember it as being very big.
    "There were lots of privet hedges and places to get lost.
However I felt that beneath the formalised structure of all this
Victoriana, there was an underlying violence which I tried to get
across in the song."

Foxtrot (album, 1972)

"I remember Paul Conroy at Charisma suggested getting
someone to dress up on stage in a red dress and a fox's head, to
promote our next record, 'Foxtrot'. I think he really fancied doing
it himself. And I thought, 'Well, damn it, if we're going to do it,
I want to do it! I want to be the centre of attention!'"

"The first gig that we tried it out was at a boxing ring in Dublin. I remember being very nervous as I walked into the stage in the middle of a number."

Supper's Ready (album track)

"There was one particular incident which gave me the inspiration for 'Supper's Ready'. There was this room at the top of Jill's (his wife) parents' house. This room was the coldest part of the house. I always used to get the shivers when I went in there.

"It was covered in strong purple and turquoise wallpaper. Everything was bright purple and turquoise. Anyway, we had this strange evening up there which ended with Jill feeling like she'd been possessed. It was extremely frightening. I don't know how to explain it – it was as if she had had a fit, or something.

"I experienced a sense of evil at that point – I saw another face in her face. I don't know how much of this was going in inside my head and how much was actually happening, but it was an experience that I could not forget and was the starting point for a song about the struggle between good and evil."

"'Supper's Ready' was a gamble. There was some resistance in the band over the length of it, people were very nervous about it. We were taking risks with stuff that we knew was likely to be uncommercial, which wasn't guaranteed to get radio-play and which was probably going to get knocked in reviews."

"At times I really felt that I was being led, for there were a number of odd coincidences. Unlikely facts would suddenly come to light, or names would suddenly lead me to other things. I ended up reading Revelations in The Bible. This explains the apocalyptic bit at the end of 'Supper's Ready'. I think it was one of the first times that I felt I got a good performance out of my voice because I felt as if I was really singing from my soul – almost like singing for my life.

"I made sure there was no-one else around when I recorded my part, because I knew that (a) I couldn't do some of the vocals very well and also I would be rather self-conscious, and (b) I was trying stuff that I knew some of the others wouldn't like. I knew that the keyboard solo was too long for the number. It was detracting. There was a great solo in there, but it needed editing. I thought that the only way that I could keep this number working was to get a vocal in. I worked for a long time to get it right.

"When the band came in – and they came in together, thank God, I made sure of that! – and I played them the tape, sure enough, Tony was outraged that I'd gone over his sacred solo. However, the rest of the band were really excited by what I'd done and popular vote was always the deciding factor. These were the absurd manipulating tactics which we were all guilty of – but probably me, more than any other!"

Willow Farm (Part 5 of Supper's Ready)
"I'm a great believer in mumble-jumble sense. I prefer things to give an air of meaning, rather than meaning itself. You can't look for meaning in some of the lyrics, they just present an atmosphere."

Peter and Phil Collins.

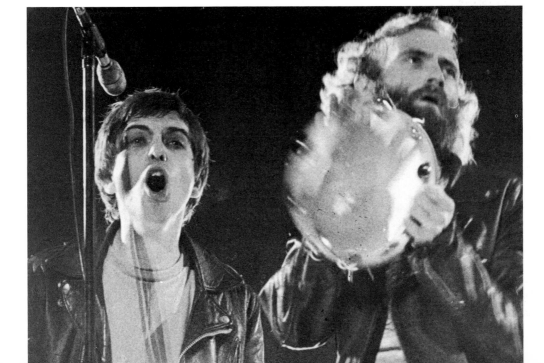

Selling England By The Pound (album, 1974)

"We were conscious of America at that time because I remember thinking that we were going to get knocked in England for slanting stuff towards America, which was partly why I wanted the title 'Selling England By The Pound'."

'Dancing With The Moonlit Knight' (album track)
"Genesis could have done R&B well. Some of our riffs could have been a lot blacker like 'Dancing With The Moonlit Knight', and sometimes we tried for that feel but by the very nature of the way we play it still comes across as being British." (1977)

I Know What I Like (In Your Wardrobe) (single/album track)
"We'd always tried to avoid writing hits, which may sound a really dumb thing. Actually now, I think it was *really* dumb. Tony played that melody line, and although I didn't think it was a great melody line, I knew people would like it.

"Their verse, I think, is good. I don't dislike the chorus but I felt, at the time, that it was taking the easy way. We did have these very high ideals about trying to do things a different way, avoiding clichés wherever possible. Although we did secretly borrow from people at different times."

The Battle Of Epping Forest (album track)
"I felt that I had a responsibility to try and steer us towards being more accessible. I really got carried away with the lyrics for 'Battle Of Epping Forest'. I enjoyed writing them but they didn't fit the music and by that point it was too late in the day.

"What happened was that I insisted on doing most of the words as I thought I could do them better than the others – which, I think, was true. The problem was that I was incredibly slow, so that, often, by the time they saw the lyrics, they would have done their parts. The backing tracks would be complete but there were no melodies and no words."

The Lamb Lies Down On Broadway (album, 1974)

"The only other idea that was seriously considered was *The Little Prince* which Mike was in favour of – a kids' story. I thought that was too twee. This was 1974; it was pre-punk but I still thought we needed to base the story around a contemporary figure rather than a fantasy creation. We were beginning to get into the era of the big, fat supergroups of the Seventies and I thought, 'I don't want to go down with this Titanic'."

"Several ideas for the album were presented in order for the band to exercise a democratic vote. I knew mine was the strongest and I knew it would win – or, I knew that I could get it to win."

"Once the story idea had been accepted we had all these heavy arguments about writing the lyrics. My argument was that there aren't many novels which are written by a committee. I wrote indirectly about lots of my emotional experiences in 'The Lamb' and so I didn't want other people colouring it. In fact there are parts of it which are almost indecipherable and very difficult which I don't think are very successful.

"In some ways it was quite a traditional concept album – it was a type of *Pilgrim's Progress* but with this street character in leather jacket and jeans. Rael would have been called a punk at that time without all the post-'76 connotations. The Ramones hadn't started then, although The New York Dolls had, but they were more glam-punk. 'The Lamb' was looking towards *West Side Story* as a starting point.

"I don't think of it that much as me, but I suppose it is. There were scenes I used from dreams that I had. But the character I was trying to create was of a different background, way of thinking, way of life than me."

"I won't feel fulfilled until it's a film. Every instinct I have tells me that the images are incredibly potent but the full strength hasn't come out yet. I've talked before about this Disneyland concept of having the audience live through the story. I want them to feel it, so say 'I remember the time when I had bodies of these soft sensual snake creatures crawling over me, I remember the time I was trapped in the cave in this claustrophobic situation, I remember seeing my brother drowning and having to decide if I was going to give myself up to attempt a rescue'. I want to actually reach through their skin, put my dirty little hands around their guts and pull them into it so it's all stored in emotional memory cells packaged in the honeycombs of their brains."

"I left Genesis after 'The Lamb Lies Down On Broadway', which was the first attempt by a rock artist to do a multi-media thing, and I've always always wanted to do that. But I was very aware at the time that my reputation as an artist was more as a wearer of flowers than as a musician. So I decided to spend some years in a visual wilderness to get the musical foundation sorted out."

Carpet Crawlers (single/album track)
"There's an art to (writing pop songs). I always thought the melody of 'Carpet Crawlers' was one of the choicest things I'd written. To me, that was a pop song." (1977)

Solo Albums & Singles

Peter Gabriel (first album, 1977)

"A lot of my new stuff is very emotional. Genesis wasn't a platform for personal songs, you couldn't have a good dose of self-pity. I'll probably record an album soon, but there won't be any heavy sell solo career and I'm not going on the road yet because that would defeat a lot of the object I left the band for."

"People tell me how melodic my album is, but to me melodies with Genesis were always very strong." (1977)

Solsbury Hill (single/album track)
"It's strange that 'Solsbury Hill' is a single because at one point it wasn't going to be on the album. I'm pleased with it especially from a *feel* point of view. It's got a kick time and that 7/4 feel works well because it feels like a normal rhythm but isn't *quite* right… a bit odd." (1977)

Here Comes The Flood (album track)
"I was referring to a mental flood, actually. You know, a release, a wash over the mind, not necessarily the land. A downhill course which leads to disaster – an opening up, a telepathic society where people can read each others' minds. Of course, in such a situation there'd be no real change for people who have been honest and open with whatever's in their minds, but those who have been rather two-faced and who have kept their thoughts hidden would find it very difficult." (1977)

Peter Gabriel (second album, 1978)

"I refuse to see it as anything other than a pop album. That's what I went in to make, and that's what it is." (1978)

"Sometimes (producer Robert Fripp) wanted to get things done very fast, which I was in agreement with, but there's a certain amount of experimentation which I like to do which he wasn't as inclined to…" (1979)

"The playing on the album is very hard edges. There's actually more synthesiser on the second album but it's used in a different way. It's used less like a string section. On the next one I want to try a couple of things built up entirely from synthesisers." (1979)

"I think Robert had seen my situation with Bob Ezrin on the first album and was consciously trying to do the very opposite. His role was more in the way of suggesting ways of doing things. I think the dryness of it was something he was very keen on as I was."

"I am concerned that people think that there are no obvious singles on the album. I thought possibly that there were one or two potential ones there…I don't know. I still believe in 'DIY' commercially."(1978)

"My first album took a couple of years to do, and there was one hit single of it, 'Solsbury Hill'. There were none from the second album. I realised that having a career in this business, there are going to be downs as well as ups." (1990)

Mother Of Violence (album track)
"I was just sitting in front of the television, stuffing myself with junk food, trapped in this negative frame of mind. I think of myself as an optimist with pessimistic tendencies, and that was one of the days when the tendencies were coming out."

DIY (single/album track)
"There was a variety of things. I think when people don't control what they do then they get no satisfaction from it. That was the simple part of it. Also I wanted to have some energy of some of the new music coming through. I wanted to in some way make reference to that, but without apeing the style in any way, which is partly why I chose the acoustic arrangement." (1979)

Indigo (album track)
"It's down and it's up. It was supposed to be just a straight situation of a father dying in a house. I had the mood of 'Old Man River' in my head at the time. And although that is a protest song there's warmth in that song which is very helpful, I think. The father was coming to terms with his imminent departure."

Home Sweet Home (album track)
"I think what frightens you is that you can't understand what drives people to do it. I really didn't want Gary Gilmore to be executed. That really got to me. The Jonestown suicide also got to me in a similar way. I suppose I must in some way feel threatened by the fact that people are prepared to take their lives."

"But within that there was perhaps a more cynical approach with life insurance and the Country and Western steel guitar." (1979)

Peter Gabriel (third album, 1980)

"It was supposed to come out in February, and the problem
was that the American label, Atlantic, heard it and didn't like it.
They called it 'commercial suicide' and there and then decided to
drop me from their label. And unfortunately, instead of sending
the record back to me, they sent it to Charisma and they have
since made a new deal with Mercury Records. You see, Charisma
wanted to set up the new American deal before they released
the album because they prefer simultaneous worldwide release
otherwise they may have problems with imports. So they held it
up for a few months. Besides that, I still had to do a few remixes."
(1980)

"Some people had other commitments and so I had to find
replacements for certain tracks. Tony Levin was only able to do
one track because he was working on a film, so most of the bass
playing was done by John Giblin from Brand X. Phil Collins did a
couple of drum tracks when Jerry Marotta went back to the States.
Guitar is mainly by David Rhodes from Random Hold and there
are bits from Fripp, Paul Weller and Dave Gregory." (1980)

"With a lot of the tracks on the album I began writing from the
rhythm first. Normally I approach them with chords and melody
and perhaps lyrics; but this album I had a small electronic drum
machine on which I used to set up rhythms and on this track
there's a 'ba ba ba ba ba ba bum – ba ba ba ba ba ba bum'. So I
would keep that as a consistent flowing pattern then the song was
written around it, and then the lyrics were really developing from
the sort of insistent almost manic qualities of that drum box... erm,
self control – states of mind ..." (1980)

"Mainly I had the rhythm first. Usually I have chords, lyrics and melodies to start with. This time I used a £60 little programmable drum machine, which is very different from the usual drum machines, and I programmed in various rhythms myself which gave me endless patterns to work on. I then wrote the lyrics on top of that followed by synthesizers and so on.

   "Then I tried other arrangements and built it up in layers and sometimes we would build up a whole arrangement and then in the studio decide to scrap a lot of the instruments. For instance, on 'Normal Life' there were about 15 tracks of music going on and we wiped most of them leaving two or three tracks at a time. So you have a certain amount of creative arrangement going on at the mixing stage." (1980)

"It was like two months of solid work but spread over a six month period. But for me the result of this approach of rhythm in the writing, using the rhythm track first, is a little revolution for me and has provided me with lots of ideas. Besides that, my taste changes over the years." (1980)

"Paul (Weller) was actually working in the next studio at the Townhouse and there was one track which we couldn't get the right guitar feel on at the time and Paul was able to go straight to it. We were looking for a certain rhythm pattern that Paul was very good for. The way he plays that rhythm stuff is amazing; he's got this sort of liquid energy in him and in the way he plays. Robert Fripp, as far as lead guitar goes, is my favourite. I think I was lucky with this album to get the best musicians around." (1980)

Peter joins in the Tom Robinson Band on stage at The Bottom Line Club in New York.

"Sometimes. I think the sound of the word is very important and the fact that I was fitting some of the lyrics to the rhythm meant that they were perhaps more conscious of the rhythm than previous albums." (1980)

"I think the lyrics are still very important on the album because they create atmospheres. That's really what I think this album is about… it's about moods and atmospheres, less specific meanings and melodies in some cases." (1980)

"I composed it starting with a drum machine and the other instruments build up on it and whatever we didn't need we just scrapped. It was also very spontaneous at times, and that produced some great ideas." (1980)

The sleeve artwork: "It was a technique pioneered by an American, Les Crims, and he called it 'Charismagraph'. Basically, as this film from an anonymous instant camera shoots out at you, you put it down in front of you and squish it for 10 minutes while it settles.
  "We all had a go at it. I did some with keys, pencils. I originally came across it in a sort of bookstore devoted to photography in a village in New York; and there was this humorous little book by Les Crims where he had some very crude and jokey designs using this technique. I gave it to Storm at Hipgnosis as a Christmas present and he in turn suggested developing that to use on the face for this album sleeve." (1980)

Biko (single/album track)
"I identify with Steve Biko quite strongly. I think he seemed very able and articulate and an intelligent youth leader. Maybe he could have been a world youth leader rather than just a black African and I was really shocked when I heard that he had been killed. And you know, normally I am not a political person but this was just something that I did want to write about. I wrote that song, or rather the information in my book, some three years ago, and when I started getting these sort of African rhythms it seemed appropriate. Then I did a lot of research on him and the song was completed." (1980)

"Bagpipes for an African song, everyone thought it was a risky mix on my part. But I've always found that this instrument has something very African about it. I checked up with some musicologists and I finished by learning that the instrument in fact had an oriental origin and not at all northern. Which gave more reason to my un-Scottish conception of the pipes." (1989)

Games Without Frontiers (single/album track)
"It was about *It's A Knockout* basically. I was really pointing out the almost childish activities of these adults behaving in such a way by trying to be the best nation in the competition." (1980)

"It was written before the Olympic Games thing blew up and I think that a lot of people assumed it was some reference to that; but it does mean that sort of aggressive, somewhat childish behaviour in adult costume and some territorial battles which take place, not merely on that TV programme but in other situations as well."(1980)

No Self Control (single/album track)
"Yes it does show an emotional state of mind… almost depressing. But I'm not always like that." (1980)

"There's some textures there which I heard on Steve Reich's 'Music for Eighteen Musicians' album with sort of voice and marimba which I like very much and tried to use some of that colour in the song. So that's a definite example of direct influence…" (1980)

Ein Deutsches Album (album, 1980)

"I've done a German version of my own album. I'm singing them in German. There is a variety of reasons. I think first and foremost you are very aware sometimes when you play in other countries that people aren't understanding what you're singing about. So if you are spending a lot of time trying to work on ideas and images and maybe 70% of the people only hear the sound and not get the ideas, then you are not getting through; you are not communicating.
    "Secondly, I found that on the last two tours I had one song, 'Me And My Teddy Bear', that I sang in German and in French which the people really liked. They appreciate the effort of an English-speaking person trying to come towards them, even though maybe I sung them badly in their language and you risk making a fool of yourself in their language. But they liked the gesture.
    "Thirdly, the language itself. Say in Germany there aren't that many groups who sing in German outside Nina Hagen and Udo Lindenberg. Also because I am English and I don't understand everything that I sing, I approach some of the words as a sound and play with the words in a way that maybe a natural-speaking German wouldn't understand." (1980)

"Because the music is a bit difficult I think the language might bring the lyrics closer to the people so that it gives the music a chance to be heard. I hope it works out."

"It's fairly close to a direct translation. There were some images which didn't work. The guy who translated it for me was Horst Kernichstein, who's done some work with Udo Lindenberg. He's very good and would explain to me why he thought certain images wouldn't translate well in German or he'd suggest what would work with a rhyme and if I felt they were wrong for the meaning then he would change them and work again. But it turned out as we wanted."

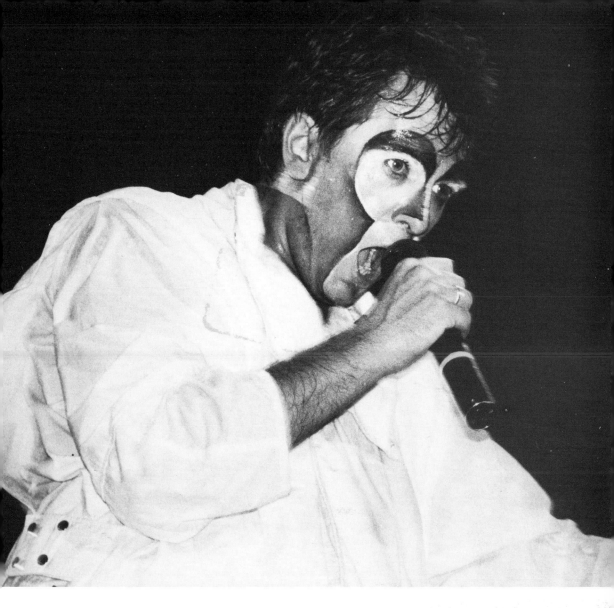

"I've spoken to Phonogram in a few territories and the only
country that was interested (in a translation) was Germany.
The French aren't interested. I was also interested in doing it in
Japanese, Portuguese and Spanish and there is still hope that I
maybe do it in Japanese. You see I don't understand Japanese at all
so I would be very reliant on the translation. So maybe I do it or
maybe not."

Peter Gabriel (fourth album, 1982)

"I have some tunes like 'I Go Swimming' and 'Milgram's 37' that
I did on this last tour and will definitely be on the next album, and
they are very similar to what I have done on this one. There is a
track called 'Twilight Zone' and 'Come My Way'... and these are
half recorded and will be on my next album around Christmas."
(1980)

"If I don't find a suitable producer then I might do it myself, but at
the moment I am like at the learning stage." (1980)

Lay Your Hands On Me (album track)
"The song was about trust, about healing and sacrifice. It's been
misconstrued, with reviews saying that I'm acting like Jesus Christ,
and that's not what I'm trying to do with that at all. I feel I am
trying to gradually involve the audience emotionally with what we
are doing with the music. I feel it's an offering of trust to the
audience. Clearly it is a dramatic moment which is contrived, in a
way; I am not denying that. But I think the effect is strong because
really what an artist is trying to do is engage the viewer, the
audience, the listener in what they are doing and get them to feel
and become part of the experience and not separated from it.
I think it really works like that, it does help bring people in."

"I feel that at times I should be of use to people. What I like in
other people's work is things that make me think about what I am
doing – gives me an awareness of something I didn't know about
before, activates my conscience, my imagination, or my spirit, and
I think when what I do is working well and is pure, then other
people can use it in that way. So partly that is what I am trying to
do with 'Lay Your Hands On Me'. I really do try and get a picture
before I go into the audience of the circle around all the people.
So there are images going through my head at that point, some of
which I feel happy to talk about, others I don't. I am not trying to
dominate that moment, I am trying to serve it."

Birdy – Music from the Film by Peter Gabriel
(soundtrack album, 1985)

"Film music is still something I'm a real novice at, but with
Birdy I was nursemaided through and it was really exciting to see
how your perception of even the dialogue could be changed
according to what soundtrack you put with it. Music is actually
a whole dimension of meaning in film, which I hadn't really
appreciated before. Also I'm trying to learn more and more myself
about making good visual images, so it's important to be able to
work with really good directors." (1987)

Peter with Sandra Bernhardt (left) and Laurie Anderson at the 1986 New Music Awards in New York.

So (1986)

"When I completed the *Birdy* soundtrack I wanted my focus to shift to songs rather than to remain on rhythm and texture, which were dominant on 'Gabriel 4'. Having done a complete album of textures and sound with 'Birdy', I'd got that out of my system." (1986)

"I wanted to be more playful, a bit more open, less mystery… It was a dark period for me and one in which I had to become a little more open to the world."

"Creation as therapy, both the fact and the gentle endorsement of that, is a thread in the material on 'So'."

"'So' was much more direct emotionally than much of my earlier work." (1987)

Don't Give Up (single/album track)
"I started off on that song singing both the parts myself but I thought it would work better with a man and a woman singing, so I changed the lyrics around. At one point I tried to work it up in a gospel-country style, and there are still echoes of that approach in Richard Tee's piano-playing." (1986)

In Your Eyes (album track)
"It's a love song. There is a tradition in Africa that intrigued me; that of writing love songs so they can be heard as love of God or the love between men and women. No one seems to do that in western lyrics, so I thought I would try mixing images. The eyes are clearly a focus point for the soul."

"For me there is a real joy with 'In Your Eyes', and I think some of that comes through to the audience. If you really want to beam in anyone, who they are or what they are, you can do so through their eyes, and so that is acknowledging that. But I am not trying to put myself over as the preacher."

"'In Your Eyes' had to be really edited, and I think it lost quite a bit as a result." (1990)

Big Time (single/album track)

"'Big Time' is a satirical story about a basic human urge.
A small man from a small town achieves all his ambitions, with all parts of his life, personality and anatomy growing larger than life, and consequently very heavy. In America, which is still a vigorous and enthusiastic nation, success has reached religious significance. This drive for success is a basic part of human nature – and my nature."

Sledgehammer (single/album track)

"This is an attempt to recreate some of the spirit and style of the music that most excited me as a teenager – Sixties soul. The lyrics of many of these songs were full of playful, sexual innuendo and this is my contribution to that songwriting tradition. Part of what I was trying to say was that sometimes sex can break through barriers when other forms of communication are not working too well.

"There is a phrase by Nietzsche about what constitutes a good book, which he said should be 'Like an axe in a frozen sea'. That triggered me off to think of tools, not to put too fine a point on the word. Obviously there was a lot of sexual metaphor there. I was trying to write in the old blues tradition, much of which is preoccupied with mating activities. The idea was the sledgehammer would bring about a mini-harvest festival."

"I knew that by using any brass at all I would invite comparisons with Phil, but Atlantic and Stax soul have always been a pivotal influence on me ever since I was at school and I've always wanted to emulate them." (1986)

Red Rain (single/album track)

"Years ago I had a recurring dream. I was swimming in a swirling sea of red and black. I remember a tremendous turmoil as the sea was parted by two white walls. A series of bottles, of human shape, were carrying the red water from one wall to another, then dropping down to smash into little pieces at the bottom of the second wall. I used this for a scene in a story in which the red sea and red rain from which it was formed represented thoughts and feelings that were being denied.

"I do believe that if feelings of pain do not get brought out, not only do they fester and grow stronger but they manifest themselves in the external world. For example, if a personal storm cannot be outwardly expressed it will appear in life in events with other people – in this case in a cloudburst."

Mercy Street (album track)

"'Mercy Street' is filled with messages and imagery of dreams, and a constant search for a suitable father figure, whether it be a doctor, a priest, or God...

"While the English and Irish workers were building the railways in Brazil they used to throw wild parties to which the Brazilians were invited with the invitation 'For All'. The Brazilians assumed that the 'For All', or 'Forro' as it later became, was the name for the event and originated the rhythm on which this track was written."

That Voice Again (album track)

"There's a Byrds influence... I'd rejected 12-string (guitar) after Genesis, but I felt that ten years was long enough so I explored the sound again. The innovation of the chorus pedal has made the effect very familiar, but that still doesn't compare with two live tracks of sound reacting against each other." (1986)

Milgram's 37 (album track)

"'Milgram's 37 (We Do What We're Told)' has been around since early last year. It's what I would call a 'dark corner' and it's perhaps the only track that rests on texture and atmosphere as its key components. Most of the others are songs you could strum along with on a guitar." (1986)

Passion (soundtrack album, 1989)

"I'm very interested in doing more film music, but there seems to be so little time. Also, it can be very difficult to break through into that scene. Basically, I've done what has been offered to me and, time permitting, I'd like to do more." (1990)

"'Passion' taught me a fluidity of sound and instrumentation. I was just coming across sounds that were beautiful to work with, and I wanted to incorporate some of the things I'd learned with the approach that I've used for the last three albums." (1992)

Us (1992)

"It has been a long time, but not as long as some people make out 'cause although it was six years from 'So', it was only three years from 'Passion', and 'Passion' for me is every bit as important as any other record I do." (1992)

"It felt right and natural since the break-up of my marriage. I've been doing therapy for five years and just stopped before Christmas, and I suppose that, rather than dealing with allusion and fantasy, I thought it was time to get my hands dirty and deal with the real stuff that was going on, and the lyrics are written to reflect that." (1992)

"To write a *me*-type record is, I'm sure, very unfashionable now, but it's sort of what's going on, and I think that if you get that stuff dealt with, you can look outside more." (1992)

"Part of what I discovered (through therapy) was the bastard in me, if you like, and I was trying to get in touch with that and put it in some of the songs. I knew it was there, the lumpy bits which move around on the surface." (1992)

"'Us' was not easy to pen, despite the therapy, and there is a certain point where I don't want to write about me all the time. It gets boring when I see it in other artists." (1992)

"You can play around graphically a lot more easily the less letters you have; and 'U' and 'S' look nice; and it actually suits the record quite well because it's primarily about relationships. I mean, I started off with 23 different things, but what tended to predominate, and I realised should be the focus for the record, was personal stuff. So I ended up leaving out some of the other more social or political bits and pieces." (1992)

Peter with Sinéad O'Connor in the video for 'Blood Of Eden'.

"To me it seems a more difficult kind of record. There hasn't been a 'Sledgehammer'-type single, which makes a lot of difference. But it's sold a million in America, and we're up to something like 4 million worldwide, and for me that still seems to be in the sunny part of the patch. It would be great if a single did take off, but I'm still very pleased with how well it's done."

"As with my third album, I think it will stand up better in hindsight than perhaps it does at the time."

Blood Of Eden (album track)
"Yeah, (Sinéad's) both very soulful and emotive and what I like about her singing is she gets this beautiful, innocent, airy voice but it comes straight from the gut with no bullshit." (1992)

Digging In The Dirt (single/album track)
"It's about digging up demons which are powerful when underground but lose their power when exposed to daylight." (1992)

Album Titles

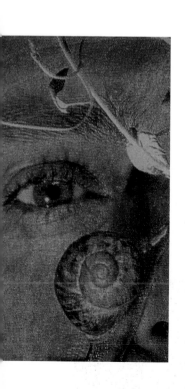

"My idea was that it should be like a magazine that appears once in a while and as with picture magazines you remember them by pictures and not by the actual contents. I thought too often groups or artists would try and present their latest work as new and startlingly different, a bit like marketing soap powder which more often than not is exactly the same as the other brand, so I thought I would make it look very similar.

"I want the albums to be something like *Newsweek* but that comes out every year... not like Daz or New Surf or whatever." (1980)

Playing Live

"All performers are paranoid egocentrics…" (1987)

"I've never quite lived up to my Fred Astaire fantasies… I'm not the most natural of movers, but it was something I wanted to know more about."

"When you get up on stage, you are in an artificial situation – you are not acting normally. Your choice of artifice then becomes the determining factor."

With Genesis

"We weren't quite dedicated enough to being on the road. Strat always used to talk about ivory towers, and he was probably right."

"I felt that we needed to get some balls into our act because I knew that we weren't cutting it. I remembered from our earlier flirtations with blues music that we'd had a certain amount of aggression which we now lacked. We changed our act so that we'd come on, as we'd always done, as polite, middle-class wimps playing melodic, inoffensive acoustic music, and then, by the end of the act, we'd launch into 'The Knife' and I'd be smashing things up and throwing cymbals around. It was as aggressive as we could get.

"We could win over virtually all the small audiences, and it was interesting to see at which point in the act they would actually be won over. It meant we were able to play the acoustic stuff with confidence, even though we had not yet played the electric.

"I used to try and wear odd stage clothes. I knew no-one else was into performing, and I would sometimes feel ashamed of the way they looked. At the same time, I knew that I wasn't going to change them, so the only thing for it was to make sure that my own performance was very powerful.

"I felt that we were failing because everyone in the group would be sitting down and not giving a shit about the audience. It was a very inward-looking attitude – that if the audience weren't able to appreciate us, they were dumb. Really arrogant!

"I think Chris Briggs, who is now an A&R man, once promoted a concert with us at Leicester University and referred to us as, 'snotty-nosed bastards' – although he later denied it. At the time, we were outraged and very hurt because he'd seemed friendly to us. But now, looking back, I can quite understand. At that time, I felt I had the difficult job, of trying to be the acceptable, human face of Genesis."

"There were good and bad gigs, but I think there was always –
even though it was often filtered or blocked – a real emotion
actually getting through. Even though we weren't getting through
to the press, we were getting through to a very mixed audience.
It wasn't just middle class music, which is how it's often portrayed
today. We were getting through to different social groups.
There were certain areas such as southern America and certain
towns in England, which were only interested in heavy music.
But, in places that were open to a few other things, I think we
began to get a foothold."

"There were points at which I felt that as a band, we all worked
very well together. The highpoints for me were the end of
'Cinema Show' and the 9/8 section in 'Supper's Ready'. I had
nothing to do with generating them, but I still felt very good about
them. There were other elements however, which troubled me.
I was still having difficulty communicating with people, particularly
if it was anything that was in some way emotional."

"When things were getting too pretty and twee and too English
public school I would try and introduce a little weirdness or
menace so that there was a darker side. It seemed as though the
aggression and weirdness would get us through when we played
gigs in more industrial areas, where I felt the prettiness seemed
rather out of place. I think the sound of the two 12-string guitars
was universally attractive but as a band we were being rejected
unless we had that darker edge."

"The audience was shocked by the weirdness of a man dressed
up in woman's clothing and a fox mask – but I loved it! This
performance gave me an unquestionable authority and I thought
'I must be on to something here'."

"We had a fantastic audience at Friars, Aylesbury. It felt like
our spiritual home. I think that was the first time that I got to the
end of 'The Knife' and started to smash things around. I got so
carried away that I jumped into the middle of the milling audience.
I hit someone as I fell and I didn't land properly. I had a horrible
sensation of something crunching. When I tried to get up I
couldn't.
    "There was so much adrenalin pumping round my body that
I didn't really feel any pain. I was lifted back on the stage, and
although I couldn't stand up, I carried on singing. I thought I'd
just twisted something. At the end of the number, the rest of the
band walked off and I was left there. People obviously thought,
'Oh, he's hamming it up a bit tonight. The old James Brown
fainting routine'.
    "By now the pain was incredible and I had to frantically
signal to people in the wings to come and help me off. I'd broken
my ankle."

"I look forward to small amounts of it (touring). I don't want to spend more than three months a year on the road, because I think that's a waste of my time now. I think I've paid my dues there. I think it's very important to do some (touring), and you get a very direct and instant judgement on what you're doing from an audience which you certainly don't get through records. I like to do it but not too much. You see a lot of sort of adult brains by-passing airports." (1980)

Solo

"It was funny the first night I went running out into the audience. Our roadie, Chip, was sent out to look after me and make sure I got back onto the stage, and one of the house security men saw this guy following me and thought he was trouble.

"They bopped him. There was our security man, being beaten up by the house security man, while I was poncing away, totally unaware of what was going on. A few nights I didn't think I'd get back on stage, and I've doubled my life insurance. At some places the audiences have been very polite, stayed in their seats and shook my hand. At other places they mobbed me. But I think if you stay on stage and seem to be above the audience, that invites much more aggressive tendencies. But if you walk around being vulnerable, then people are very friendly. I'm not putting over any big superstar thing so there's nothing to hit out at. At least that's what I tell myself as I go in wearing my bullet-proof vest!" (1977)

Supporting Frank Zappa in Berlin in 1980

"People were throwing stuff at me, wanted to punch me. There was a guy yelling, 'English Pig, Go Home!' I crawled up on stage and started to do 'Here Comes The Flood', which was literally the quietest number I had at that point, and that didn't work either. I walked off.

"It was my worst night ever as a performer. Up until then I'd always been afraid of it happening. Now it had happened. Once the hurt and the shock wore off, I began to adopt a different frame of mind. After a day's break, the next show was in Bremen with Zappa, and even though it wasn't going over again, I felt relaxed, intact. I began laughing and feeling at home, and the crowd responded. In the end, we did much better – it still wasn't fantastic – but I'd overcome my fear of being challenged, of being rejected by an audience." (1980)

"Because most concerts are a part of long tours, people think, well, this is going to be the same if I see it in ten days' time or two months' time. And as soon as you involve the audience you introduce the unpredictable. You cannot know for certain when I am going to get back to the stage, what's going to happen to me down there, and so I think it keeps things interesting."

"When you sit down there and you watch some shows, you get the feeling that you are watching a very rehearsed band who know exactly what they are doing. Well, our policy is to provide the opposite of that. And to that effect there are a few new numbers which as yet have no words and no melody and a few loose ends and we are playing these in slowly. This is one of those and it may give you an opportunity to watch us mess up. I hope you enjoy it."

"I'm gonna try and get to a lot of countries too that aren't normally on the rock'n'roll circuit, 'cause I think the Human Rights Now tour was an incredible experience for all the musicians taking part, and many of us were playing a lot of places that hadn't had many concerts before, certainly of that scale. I think a lot of us are now gonna try and include Africa, India, Central-South America, Eastern Bloc etc… The problem obviously is then getting to pay for it, because the economies and the amount you can charge for tickets is much less than in the rich countries; but it means so much to the people and it's very interesting so I'm looking forward to it." (1992)

"For about ten years now I've been trying to put together a sort of video tour, with massive screens which we're gonna move around and do different things; and in a sense that way has been incredibly well forged by U2, but that is good for me, as now it's a good challenge and we're gonna steer it quite a lot differently." (1992)

"It's usually into the mouth of the dragon facing the critics in London. It's a colder climate here, too. In Italy the audiences are very outgoing, singing along to every song, and then suddenly you get to Britain, and it's much more polite and reserved, and you have to work that much harder." (1993)

"I wanted to break some new ground with this show. I was originally planning an all out video assault, with flying screens and stuff, but then I saw the U2 Zoo TV tour in America – I saw it five times actually – and the visual intelligence there was so strong that I thought maybe I shouldn't be trying a video spectacular, I should be trying something else." (1993)

"I'd originally got an idea for a big video thing and I wanted to find some way of getting video images to move around on stage. But although it was quite a different idea to what U2 did (on the Zoo TV tour), I felt that they'd got that video-music territory well carved out; I really enjoyed that show, and I thought it was done with quite a lot of wit and intelligence. So I thought I should move in another direction." (1993)

"I think Robert (Lepage, set designer) is his generation's Peter Brooke. He does very simple things, which are almost gags, but which have a real emotional starkness to them. He felt most of what I was writing about was transformation, hence the idea of two stages to integrate the polarities, male-female, man-made organic, fire-water." (1993)

"When I left Genesis (in 1975), I was known and the group was known almost as much for our visuals as for our music, certainly in a live context. So when I set out on my solo career, I wanted to put the music on a firm foundation before I got too far into the visual. It's taken a little longer than perhaps I reckoned, but I felt the time had now come to try and break some new ground with the show side of it." (1993)

"If you absorb the images as they come at you, hopefully some of them will have an afterlife, and resonate a little. The sense I've got back from people is that the music and the imagery are coming from the same place, that they haven't been artificially stuck together." (1993)

"I was always optimistic about this tour (1993). There were always pessimists among us, doubts whether everything would work. But I did not share them. I did have the riot act read to me from time to time. But when you've got something set up in your head, it's very hard to cut it down." (1993)

"With this show (1993) we're trying to hit halfway house between theatre and rock'n'roll. It isn't easy. It's an ongoing process. Theatre people and rock people don't always talk the same language. But I just wanted to break some new ground." (1993)

Conspiracy of Hope Tour 1986

"That tour was my training ground. I'd done a couple of press
conferences in Genesis days and decided I didn't like them or
function well in them. But I'm a lot less nervous than I used to be
and press conferences are a lot easier when you're selling something
which your ego is not completely wrapped up in, something which
you believe in." (1989)

"San Francisco felt like a whistle-stop on a presidential election
campaign, the sense of excitement, and then we were meeting
the former prisoners of conscience on the tour including a Chilean
woman, Veronica De-Negri, whose son had just gone back home
and been burned to death in the street by police – they'd poured
petrol over him and set fire to him. I was just churning inside with
these different emotions. Adrenalin carried me through that first
one. Since then I've improved. The thing is it's a performance.
You need to be clear about what you want to say and put it across
in a strong and forceful way, very concisely and with some
emotion." (1989)

1988 Tour

"What I remember most is changing faces, Japanese faces, Indian
faces with turbans bobbing up and down, Greek faces, African
faces. All within a few days." (1989)

Sting, Tracy Chapman, Bruce Springsteen,
PG and Youssou N'Dour.

"Bruce (Springsteen) is Mr America in many ways and that Coca-Cola culture is incredibly insular, but he was struggling with the languages, listening to the local music, and studying the politics of each country as we went along. He's got a real big heart, that was very clear." (1989)

"Everyone pulled their weight and the whole tour was a colossal achievement. We travelled together, we plotted together. I got elected to do a few of the dirty jobs. There were lots of little political jobs. There were lots of little political flash fires – a delicate balance of large egos all round. I'm not sure whether I'm good at it, but part of me likes it." (1989)

"The cultural boycott of South Africa is something I have a lot of problems with. For instance, I don't have my records released in South Africa and Tracy (Chapman) does. I support 100 per cent the argument that art has always been connected with cultural change so that if you cut off artistic communication you slow the process down. However, I do support the boycott, although I think it's wrong, because we are asked to by the people involved, the black people of South Africa. I took the decision out of respect for their struggle." (1989)

"The dilemma was there throughout, but particularly when we had a black audience. In Harare the black musicians we discussed it with said that we should just go along with the normal machinations of the music business and that it would be racist to make changes because of the colour of the artist and the audience." (1989)

"I'd been leaving it out (the backward freefall into the audience) because it feels like an unfair card to play when it's not my own show. In that package we were trying to put across a message and my drop can look like a very ego-driven moment, although that's not my motivation. But in Abidjan… white performers, black audience, you know, to surrender yourself seemed important to me. In fact I didn't get passed around as I normally do because the security guys, who'd been trying to persuade me not to do it, hung on to my legs the whole time. But it was the same as anywhere else really. A nice feeling. People tend to be pretty gentle."

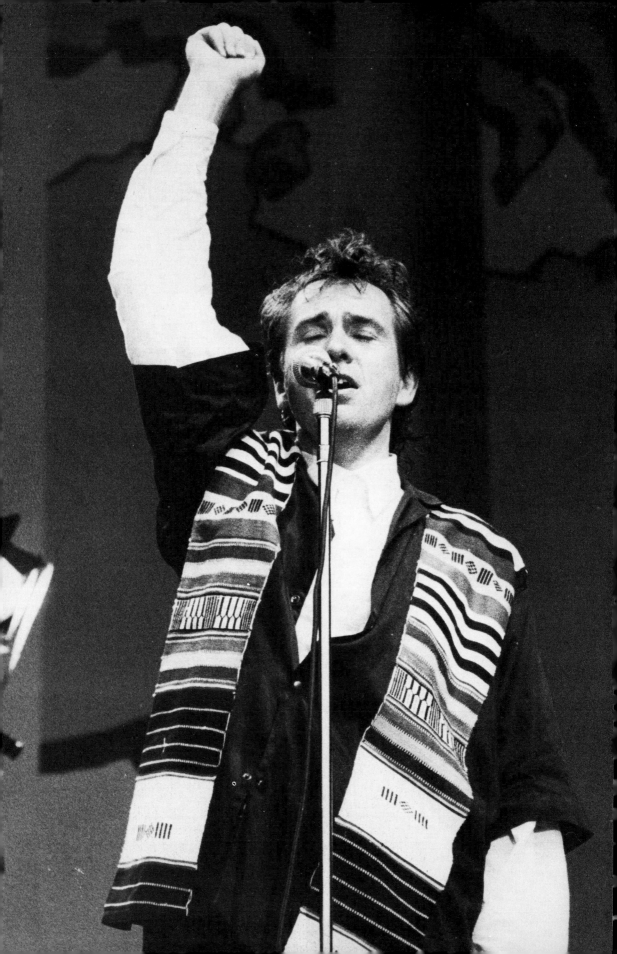

World Music

WOMAD

"WOMAD started in 1980, and towards the end of the Seventies a few of us had been starting to listen to some music from other countries. I think there was a friend of mine who was a journalist in Bristol and we were both failed drummers, but we were getting turned on by some of these wonderful rhythms we were hearing – and then melodies and vocal things, and passionate performances. And at that time I think there were maybe two record stores in London that carried that type of music – World Music, as it's now known – and it was very hard to see events. We started to try to put an event together. We have some moments now where you take over the whole centre of the town, and you walk down little streets and in each square there's a small stage, and different foods from different countries. And that's the format I particularly like the best." (1993)

"The beginning was a lumpy, bumpy start, and that was partly in that we were full of idealism and not enough practicality in those days. Enough people said, 'there's never gonna be enough interest in World Music, there's a very cynical world out there, no-one wants this stuff anyway'. Fortunately that's been proved wrong and WOMAD is now functioning in 14 countries, but the first one lost a lot of money, and it was only through Genesis' generosity that there was a benefit concert, that gave us the wherewithal to continue. I've not been involved in the management organisation side since the first one, except as a peripheral adviser, and now as a participator in Real World Records." (1992)

"I was getting very excited by some of the things I was coming across. So I thought, if they are so exciting to me, I'm sure they will be interesting to a lot of other people too. So I was sitting on a train one evening and I thought, wouldn't it be great to have an

event which could bring in a large audience with a few rock and roll groups, and have that audience exposed to a lot of this stuff."

"I felt that an important influence on music over the next few years will be ethnic in origin and I can hear it being combined with electronics and more expressive, emotive use of the synthesizer. Also I have been listening to and enjoying some of the recent material by Talking Heads who seem to be in that area and the tape made by David Byrne and Brian Eno. What I am actually trying to do with some of this stuff is to sift out rhythms which have a clarity and a simpleness to them. I think that much of the Afro-rock and Afro-influenced music of the past had tended to use the more complex rhythms which I find less interesting."

"We started talking to people and the whole process of finding the music was like a detective trail. It was a very potent idea and the further we went into it the more it became clear that if we were going to go to the trouble of assembling people from elsewhere it would be a good idea to do it with more than just African groups. And that in terms of logistics and cost it would have to be more than an indoor venue because it became quickly clear that finance and backing was not readily available."

"There are two jobs to be done. One is protect and preserve the seed stock of as wide and varied a base as you can keep alive. The other is to try out as many hybrid possibilities as you can that will give you the most vibrant, pulsating new life forms. Hopefully, the WOMAD festivals in America will reflect this mixture of ancient and modern."

"...inform and excite and to make a wide audience aware of the worth and potential of a multicultural society by promoting the music, arts and dance of many different cultures, both traditional and contemporary."

"Although I'm no longer involved in WOMAD on a direct level I keep in touch. Things are very much hand to mouth and it's a real struggle but it's still growing..." (1987)

"WOMAD is one way of fighting racism. Kids are growing up listening to black music, seeing black faces on the street and generally getting into what they're getting into. That's one way... to minimise wide-scale prejudice and allow the blacks to become doctors, architects and policemen – professional people, and not just letting them concentrate on sport and music which they know they can do." (1984)

"As most of our music comes from a black culture, to be a rock musician and a racist is a direct contradiction."

The First Festival (1982)

"It was a wonderful turning point for me, despite the dark side. There was a sense of a pivotal event which was fantastic for the people who were there. We were naïve in that we were in a missionary state of extreme excitement and zeal and when you get swept away like that you're prone to being over-ambitious. But it was a bold experiment. In truth, all the gut instincts were correct, we were just a little ahead of our time." (1989)

"We started to realize things were collapsing during the event. There were concerns before then, but we were confident we were going to get a much bigger audience than we had. We had the rail strike against us, and we had appalling publicity, which was a pity because I thought it was ideal colour supplement material."

Peter with Youssou N'Dour.

The Collapse

"We had been fired up by our own imagination and enthusiasm and thought everybody else would be. Of course it happened a few years later but at the time we consequently ran into big debts that were beyond my resources… The experience made me perhaps a little more worldly-wise and more cautious. I've not been involved in the management of WOMAD since then, except as an external adviser." (1992)

"Because I wasn't working on it full-time I didn't want to tell the WOMAD people how to do it. Some of the pros in the business were very sceptical and cynical about the whole thing, Gail (Colson – Peter's manager at the time) particularly, saying, 'This isn't going to work and blah blah blah.' We were saying, 'Oh yes it is. People will like this idea'. We were very confident and naïve. But I didn't want to come on the big rock star, 'You've got to do it this way. This is the way things are done'. I think I was a bit stupid in that way. I should have been more aggressive. I had no idea I was going to be seen as the only one worth chasing as things went down."

"When the shit hit the fan, people identified me as the only fat cat worth jumping on so I got the aggro, a lot of flak, nasty calls. I didn't have that kind of money available at the time though and I'd lost quite a lot of money already." (1989)

"(Wife) Jill actually got a death threat aimed at me, an anonymous caller saying, 'I'm going to kill you afterwards', and all that stuff, very nasty. Not the sort of thing I want to live through again."

"They'd done such a fantastic job I couldn't let them go down the tube. Although to the people in the Gabriel money camp, it came at exactly the wrong moment…" (1993)

Third World Music and Musicians

"Whatever corner of this planet you happen to be born in, you should have equal opportunity to get yourself heard and seen in terms of music, arts and politics." (1993)

Peter on stage with Ugandan songwriter
Geoffrey Oryema.

"Wonderful music, I think. I mean they are extraordinarily gifted
but I also love the colours that it provides for the music. I've always
enjoyed records that have landscapes that feel like new territory,
where some of the elements have been put together in a different
way, even though they may be themselves familiar." (1992)

"Well, some of it's by design and planning, and some of it's
chance, and is being led by whoever happens to be visiting the
studio, or WOMAD, who has this world music festival just across
the river from us; so sometimes I just see some interesting people
across the road and if I know what they're doing I'll suddenly
think, 'maybe that will be great on this song'." (1992)

"I watch some of the Indian and Pakistani singers and they have
this gestural language too, and there is definitely a sense there of
energy exchange, which sounds like a post-Sixties term."

"You do get this two-way exchange now – people quite often
see it as just these white colonialists coming along and ripping off
these Third World artists, but it's actually quite a real exchange,
I think. But there's some responsibility on those of us who do take
ideas from elsewhere to help try to promote the sources of the
music.

"My own view is that if we are going to find a way to
incorporate all the races or skin colours or cultures, not just mix all
the colours up so you get one messy colour but so that it keeps
them independent.

"I think for my work as a musician, hearing a lot of this stuff has
really changed the way I write, the way I think about rhythm –
and getting the chance to work with a lot of these wonderful
performers has changed the way I perform and sing." (1993)

Making Music On His Own

First Steps

"I want to make music that's respected by my peers – so it's a matter of trying to come up with music that is satisfying to me, worthy of respect, and which ideally would appeal to a wide audience." (1986)

"It's strange – someone can write a book in seven days or seven years, and no-one grumbles. But when you're making records people complain and ask you what you were doing if you weren't part of the album-tour circuit." (1986)

"I think lots of art – it seems like a grand word, but I mean painting, music, any sort of creative activity – has some therapeutic value, and it's a means of externalizing thoughts and feelings. So I was doing it regardless, and then I got into the situation that I was in at the beginning of Genesis, of being a songwriter and not wanting to become a performer, and I was having trouble interesting people in my songs. We took the songs to a few publishers."

"We thought maybe we should try and get a hit record and sell it as a TV idea. We were looking at idiosyncratic comedians and Charlie Drake seemed like a good choice. I had sketches of this stick-insect type character that would have fitted in."

"'The Lamb' was my first attempt to do a multi-media thing, which is what I've always wanted to do. But I was very aware at that time that my reputation as an artist was more as a wearer of flowers than as a musician. So I decided to spend some years in a visual wilderness to get the musical foundation right." (1993)

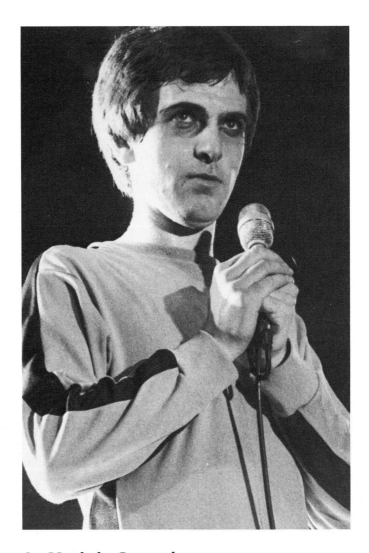

On Music in General

"I think persistence is worth more than talent in terms of achieving results. Because in a sense I think people are born talented and tend to limit themselves." (1990)

"Music and art are just languages that anyone can learn and I don't think anyone should be discouraged because they don't feel good enough."

"I hear a lot of musicians trained up to the eyeballs who haven't got the right feel – particularly when white English players are trying to get laid-back, and it doesn't quite sit. But if you can learn that on drums, focus only on rhythm and phrasing and accent, then that I think is the centre of any musical language." (1990)

Songwriting

"I think it's very important just to keep exploring because that way you keep questioning your music. Sometimes when I'm sitting at the piano I find that I would want to play things in a style which I've finished with in certain ways but then I feel 'Well, maybe don't just play the first thing that comes to mind. Think about it and maybe throw that away and try and use some of that feeling or that idea in a new approach'.

   "Often with music you just hear the final product, but there is often a lot of thought process. Like for instance, you do something and discard it and so go on until you get to the end product. When I do my own music I say 'Right this is the way people usually do it. Now is there a better way or a more interesting way that I could try?'" (1980)

"I think there are all sorts of things that provide influences. More often it's on a general level. Things that I like get stored in the memory bank, and sort of flavour stuff that comes out the other end…" (1980)

"Originally I was thinking it would take three albums to get to a point where I felt as a writer I had to establish myself." (1980)

"I think drum machines are great things for writers to work with and I find that the style of music I superimpose on the drum pattern is different from that which I would generate without it. Even though I make changes sometimes with a melody or a sound, I try and keep the rhythm as constant as possible so that your body can lock into it." (1980)

"I don't really feel part of a revolution as such. I think I'm outside of the main area. So it's a sort of gradual thing rather than in terms of old wave and new wave... I don't really belong to either. I really hate to be pigeon-holed and for me I prefer to be able to float around in the wings. When musicians get pigeonholed it becomes a problem for them because that tag stays with them for the rest of their lives." (1980)

"Craft in writing is something that, as a writer, has always interested me. We began with Genesis a long time ago as a songwriter's co-operative, and there's a lot of skill in getting good craft into a short song. The Kinks' 'Waterloo Sunset' and Randy Newman's 'I Think It's Going To Rain Today' are fantastic illustrations." (1982)

"When people feel intensely, they find a way of making their bodies respond to those feelings, articulating them as they might in a painting – those little collections and bends in notes put the soul in." (1992)

"I think ideas are like a lucky dip. You feel for shapes that are interesting and you try to guess what they are and make some sense of what they could be, then you pull them out and unwrap them and see. I don't think many of them arrive fully formed." (1992)

"It's like taking your hands and feet off the controls: this thing carries on and you carry on with it. But I do think I make my life difficult by putting up all these ideas." (1992)

On Commerciality

"Personally, I will only make the music which I want to make, and will only then go out to sell it in the best possible way that I can." (1984)

"I take the attitude that once with music, I don't compromise at all... I do exactly what I want even though it's going to be labelled 'commercial suicide' in America, but once I've finished that I'll try and sell it whatever way I can." (1980)

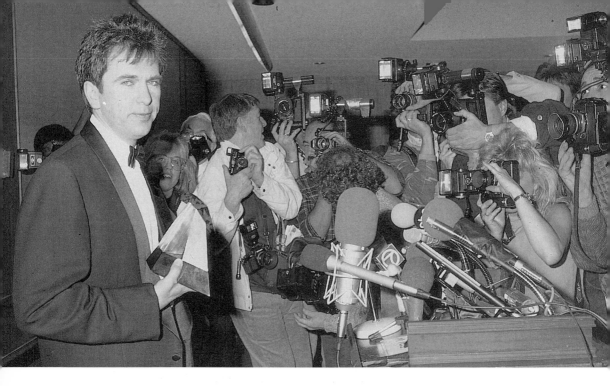

"Well, during the recording (of 'Peter Gabriel 3') one of Atlantic's A&R guys came over to get an idea of it – and besides attempting to make one track sound like The Doobie Brothers, which he failed to do, he hated the rest of the stuff and decided that he didn't want to be involved. So, as expected, when I sent them the album they ignored it and dropped me from the label." (1980)

"I think the stuff on my albums differ from each other, and even though the last album is the best I've ever made I don't want to market the albums like that. That's *stupid*." (1980)

"I've never known any musician who's been willing to live in poverty… If you decide to put a record out, you're going into a commercial market-place and you're either honest about it or you're not." (1984)

"I would rather make my sound commercial than make an album based on other commercial sounds. So first of all I just work on a thing that sounds right and then I try and sell it rather than design the music in order to sell, because I think that's a cheap way to do it and in the long run it makes uninteresting music because you would be imitating.

   "It was like when The Bee Gees started selling records, then everyone started making records like them. The Sex Pistols sold a lot of records so everybody sounded like the Pistols. It happens all the time in music, and to me it's not important to be the biggest selling artist and sell more than Abba or the Pistols or The Beatles. Sure, I want to sell records – but more important is to make music that interests me and excites me." (1980)

"I've seen a lot of people disappear after a meteoric rise. I believe I'll be going up and down for a considerable length of time. Actually media people and business people take more notice of that than the public do – which may seem surprising." (1980)

On Other Musicians

"I've tried to be totally honest in my writing, which doesn't necessarily make for the most flattering or easily digestible lyrics. One reason why I really admired John Lennon's writing was that he was honest even when it made him look bad or weak. The lyric of 'Jealous Guy' is a good example. I've tried to make my writing as real as that, and sometimes it's not the nicest thing to listen to." (1992)

"'Cold Turkey' by John Lennon was one of the first white singers' records that really grabbed me, and regardless of the subject matter it just cut right through." (1982)

"A lot has happened. The original burst of new life which we had a few years back has really been very healthy and there's been a lot of very interesting new acts emerge. It's interesting to see them develop. Each generation has its own revolutionary spearhead based on energy and excitement and that gets tempered and the musicians then begin exploring other areas." (on punk and after)

"I like The Jam a lot. They're an excellent example of a band who are going way beyond where they originally started." (1980)

"We're both 28, and we both grew up listening to the same music: The Kinks, The Yardbirds, Manfred Mann, the Stones, The Beatles…" (1979, on sometime writing partner Tom Robinson)

Peter on stage with Jim Kerr of Simple
Minds at the Nelson Mandela Concert at
Wembley Stadium.

"Pete Townshend is one of the few people with integrity
untouched in this business." (1982)

"The first time I heard Simple Minds was on the *John Peel Show*.
I was looking for a support act for the Intruder tour… The first
time I saw them on that European tour, they immediately made
me think of Genesis, the Genesis of the earliest days. I know this is
a surprising comparison but it's true. The similarity is not their
music, but the way of approaching it and exploiting it.'" (1989)

"I wanted to play before The Stranglers because they were
considered to be a 'punk band', you know, dangerous and anti-
establishment. I was interested in playing to a punk audience and
see how I'd go down with them. In the end it was fine. I went
down really well and I enjoyed it." (1990)

"I supported The Tubes at Knebworth Park at the height of their
popularity and that was fine by me. It was good for me to do that"
(1990)

"I really wanted to approach a lot of things differently in a
somewhat unorthodox fashion. And I thought it would be much
better to try using someone who was young maybe, hadn't got
fixed ideas about the right way to record a thing. And I'd liked
Steve (Lillywhite)'s work on The Banshees and XTC. So …"
(1980, on choosing a producer)

"Under New Wave there exists a large variety of musicians, most of whom look young, some of whom aren't young, doing things that people have done before. They're portrayed as musical revolutionaries whereas, in fact, they're not. For me, the only thing that was new was the use of accent which, outside of Tommy Steele records, had never been fully exploited." (1984)

"I like pop songs. Particularly Steely Dan, 10CC, those sort of people who write well-produced pop songs. Obviously The Beatles…" (1977)

"XTC and The Banshees are two other bands that I could mention. They are energetic and individually very strong." (1980)

"I like (Robert) Fripp. He's very interesting, very imaginative and a real character. I've seen his new band and it's like a sort of modern dance band and I think it should work out great for him… They're really good." (1980)

"I think Bowie is interesting and I think it's important that rock music should have people on the outside of the mainstream that are prepared to experiment and take risks." (1980)

"I am a great Springsteen fan. I was initiated in London at his second show. He'd been receiving a lot of bad press because he'd been hyped somewhat silly, and there was a lot of resentment. His PR man, who was a friend of mine, insisted that I went along to see him, Then I went along to the show very sceptical, and was totally floored.
   "I think he's one of the very few mainstream artists that combines great melodies, I mean great feel, playing, lyrics and performance. There's very few people that can do all of those things." (1982)

"Daniel (Lanois, producer) and I have incredibly strong and differing opinions – but opinions that are quite frequently reversed. Something you were prepared to kill for on Tuesday, you're ready to kill on Friday." (1992)

Guest Appearances

"I was so nervous… a session man, you know… I thought, wow! And they taped my breaths while I was nervously preparing for my little line, and made it a joke track which they all laughed at afterwards, when I'd gone." (on contributing flute to Cat Stevens' 'Mona Bone Jakon' album in 1970)

"I agreed to do it because I love The Beatles, and it was a great pleasure for me to record one of their songs. But I found that the general arrangements were not very good." (on 'Strawberry Fields Forever', his contribution to the various artists album 'All This And World War II' in 1977)

Recording &
Making Videos

"Traditionally, the studio's the perfect environment for paranoia." (1990)

"I bounce a lot of ideas off the musicians I happen to be playing with and then maybe the producer later on. I also find it useful to have someone to bounce off ideas in the writing stage as well. But as yet I haven't really used anybody." (1980)

"Once you are in the studio you get that same freshness again from each individual musician as though it was a one-piece band." (1980)

"I try to finish the right side of midnight. I started doing that when we had young kids because they tend not to be aware that you finished a session at 4am, they still jump on you at five. But I've had too much of my time in meetings recently...." (1989)

"I do enjoy maintaining a burst of energy and discipline, but mostly, when I'm working on a project, I'm juggling several others at the same time. Brian (Eno) will go into a studio and shut off everything else, just focusing completely on what he's doing. I'm thinking: 'I have to nurse this along, I have to make these phone calls...'" (1992)

"I think the studio should be capable of trapping magic whenever and wherever it appears." (1990)

"I spend a lot of time working on the sound of my records so that they will appeal to as many people as possible." (1987)

Living in the Real World –
The Studio & Label

"My advances from royalties go towards studio equipment and it gives me the opportunity to experiment and make the record the way I choose. It also means that if I want to do other, non-commercial projects it's not prohibitively expensive." (1986)

"I know world music is a fashion now and, like reggae, it may be in or out of favour at different times, but the rats are there in the stores and they're not going to go away. You know, I read this scary statistic from America that the average album is played 1.2 times. It's an impulse buy, or something to impress a girlfriend, part of the artillery with which you announce yourself to the world. Well, Real World is hoping to make records that people want to play more than once." (1989)

Peter in his Real World Studios near Bath.

"I wanted to create another new way of recording and have a sort of cellular structure around some shared facilities and shared intelligence, so I have one large acoustic studio, then a lot of control ones around the outside. Instead of having a Fairlight, Synclaviers and all the rest in each studio, you can share some of the intelligence and access it by computer from any point on the site. We would like to have five or six other artists on the site, each with a room so that it can be a functioning community."

"We have a sort of slogan for the studio, 'high tech and hand made', and that suits my philosophy." (1990)

"What I've actually created here (Real World) is very busy, and there are a lot of people wanting my time." (1992)

"We've designed the place to allow for both the best technology can offer in terms of tools and the right environment for great performance. Because if you don't have that, you've lost everything!" (1989)

"We had one session with a drummer playing right here and he saw a duck swim by underneath, then a dog chasing it, so he ran out, dived in and rescued it." (1989)

"It's not ideal, but I really like this site. I spent a lot more money than anticipated on soundproofing. We thought of putting a canopy over it like the Sydney Opera House but the estimate was twice what we could afford. I wasn't sure about the look of it at first, but I like it now. It's chunky. And a very good place to be if there's a nuclear attack. Basically, it has to be a commercial success or I'm in trouble." (1989)

"I don't know what to put in it, but their use of materials is great, lots of innovative ideas – out of necessity, I know." (1989)

"I liked the site and when I'm riding an idea I can't be shifted." (1993)

The Theme Park

"It would have to be a place where you had fun because you couldn't survive without it. If it was just serious and a place where you were challenged then it would be too much. Maybe you would involve a regular funfair in it as well."

"I picture a lot of places in the future that are a combination of holiday camp, university and art gallery. It's the way things must go. With mass unemployment, it seems there are only three solutions to the prospect of massive riots – education, entertainment or warfare. And the first two are preferable to conscription."

"It's been a fantasy and a dream, and does run the risk of being taken seriously now, which is reassuring; but it still may not happen. However, where we are is, the Mayor of Barcelona is very keen for it to happen there and we'll know, I think, within four weeks whether we have the go-ahead there.

"The aim is really to have this magical garden which is in itself a beautiful place, lots of running water, trees, calming experience, and then behind the 12 waterfalls will be doorways into these adventures underground, which will be experiences designed by the film-makers, artists, musicians, painters, psychologists, architects, whatever, that will be collaborating in such a way that you don't just go around this as a passive lump that receives, but you're active. You get inside it, you get to make decisions. I think there's an enormous range of things you can do.

"We have these crazy evenings where we, usually over food and a few glasses of wine, sit around brainstorming ideas, and Brian Eno and Laurie Anderson have now been actively involved for the last two years."

"It's a long way away because there are so many things which need to be ironed out. The idea is a multi-media, sociological, ecological wonderland – a show in which people can participate. Brian Eno is a partner in it, as is Will Alsop the architect. I started looking for a home for it in 1986 – both Sydney and Cologne have said no. Now I'm trying to see if I can arrange it for Barcelona…" (1990)

"Trying to plug our dreams into this industry is turning out to be quite an interesting marriage." (1993)

On His Record Label, Charisma

"I met this journalist in LA who told me about a band she had seen. When she sent me the tapes I just took them to Charisma to try and get their record on the label. Unfortunately Charisma got a bit carried away and went over to LA and signed them there and then and I'm not sure whether Vivabeat were ready for it…

"I tried before with Random Hold and they've been turned down by Charisma. I was looking around for things for Charisma for a while because I thought they were getting stale. Also, a week after Madness formed, this guy, whom I introduced to Charisma, came in with the tapes and Charisma weren't interested." (1980)

"I just wanted Charisma to have some foot in 1980 and not everything in 1970. There is only Genesis and me really on Charisma." (1980)

"Artists always end up having arguments with their labels at some point or another, or feel they're being ripped off by their labels. Which I should point out I don't with my labels at present…" (1990)

On Computers and Technology

"Technology is the revolution in the sense that it will change people's lives more than any other single thing in the next 50 years – much more than Marx or Hitler." (1979)

"Well I've been programming synthesisers for about two or three years now, so I'm getting the hang of it. Some of it. There's a new sort of computer based digital machine which we were exploring on this album a bit. That's very different. What's fascinating for a musician is you can put any sound into it; you can tap a glass or blow your nose, or any sound you can think of, and then the computer will analyse it, and send it back to the keyboard, so you can process it any way you like. So it gives a huge sort of capacity or huge scope.

"You have a sort of TV screen which you work with so you're working to some extent with the waveform. You have a light pen that you can program the waveform on to the screen and get a considerable amount of control over the sound like that. So as they develop the visual correspondence I think it will become easier. At the moment it does take a little time to get the hang of it, but I think it's within anyone's grasp if they have the time available." (1980)

"I think people tend to go with the first things that come through, particularly with the use of sequencers. I listened to a lecture given by Wendy, it used to be Walter Carlos, who with Larry Fast is the best in terms of sounds, and the thing that she was saying was she spent hours and hours building in little inaccuracies and little mistakes and imperfections, building up each tone with say three different sounds, each note so that by the time you listen to it at the end it sounds very human.

   "Although I like the machine effect, I think very often the electronics people don't spend enough time working on it, 'cause it is a very laborious and time consuming process. However, the end result sort of springs to life in a way that some 'bang out a pattern on a sequencer' doesn't." (1980)

"I wish I understood the equipment more. I'm what equipment manufacturers call an RFM.... Erm… 'Read the Fucking Manual'…" (1992)

"Some groups think it's hip to be cold and dispassionate, but a synthesiser has far more scope than people give it credit for. There are ways that the human personality can manifest itself by a variety of decisions that centre around that one note." (1984)

"In theory, you function differently when you're analysing things at the computer, say, or going into detail on a track, than when you're playing along, and the red light's on, the adrenalin's pumping, and it's a live performance. I call them energy 'A', analytical, and energy 'Z' which would be zen or performance, improvised, spontaneous. Two different ways of interacting with the machine." (1990)

"I think it's pretty dumb to write off CDs as belonging to yuppies. They should belong to anyone, and the price should come down to a point where there are no social connotations involved." (1987)

"There's a whole culture around future technology, the trippy end of it which I call the cyber world – virtual reality, CD-ROM and all that – which reminds me of that '60s sense you'd get from *Oz* and *IT* of wide open frontiers." (1993)

"We're a walking advertisement for Apple computers here; if only we'd managed to get to them earlier." (1993)

Videos

"If I dry up then… tough. But I have a string of other things that interest me, visual things like video discs and maybe films and stuff." (1980)

"The last time I cried was when filming my last video when a snail dug its teeth into my eyelid." (1992)

"I would like to get (Real World) set up to be ready for developing long-form video which I think will become a really exciting medium."

"We worked out the budget. If I do all of the tracks, it will cost something like $1.5 million. And the possible income, even if it's very successful, will be something like $750,000. So I have either to trim my ideas or trim the number of tracks. I don't mind not making a profit on it, but I do mind losing the money, because the studio itself is about three times as expensive as we were planning." (on a projected long-form video of 'So')

"Live shows can be pretty boring by the time they get to film. I would like to try and somehow get to represent what it is like to be in my position. Normally you have the concert as seen from the audience, it would be nice to cut away and treat the music as raw material so if you want to stop in the middle of a number and cut away to silence you can do that rather than saying the music has to stay intact." (on live video)

"I like to take my time over videos, and I've got the reputation of being something of a tortoise anyway. For me, the visual images are as important as the musical ones, and even though I bring in other people who are much more familiar with the film-making processes than I am, I still like to get involved and develop all the ideas with them. 'Sledgehammer' took a total of three weeks' work, though, and most artists aren't prepared to put that sort of time into a video." (1987)

With Kate Bush.

Solsbury Hill

"It was a little conceptual, dealing mainly with close-ups of my shoulder. And it was not greeted with enthusiasm by the record company first of all."

Games Without Frontiers

"The idea of the song was countries behaving like playground kids. It's against nationalism, but they had seen me moving around the table with the kids and thought that I was leering at them like a dirty old man. At the end there was a whole series of children's toys, and they thought that the Jack in the Box was an obvious reference to masturbation. So it says a lot more about the minds of the people who ran *Top Of The Pops* than it did about my video."

Don't Give Up

"A clinch from start to finish, that's all. I didn't fight (director Godley and Creme's) idea, but I thought that five minutes of groping Kate Bush in front of the world was perhaps not the best thing for a dodgy marriage. At the time I felt I needed… a blessing. Anyway, Jill was great about it." (1989)

"I wasn't that happy with the way it came out, but it was getting late and the single needed a video."

Sledgehammer

"At some points I was in agony. For the train sequence, which lasts ten seconds, I had to be in the same position for six hours – the track had to be built up a little bit each time, and the smoke had to be moved round as the train moved along. The fruit smelled all right after a few hours under the studio lights, but the fish stank."

"The 'Sledgehammer' video was fun and, as they say, appeals to all ages... I felt some very childish satisfaction in being the first artist to have a video with sperm in it on *Top Of The Pops*!" (1987)

Mercy Street

"The video for 'Mercy Street' hasn't been seen very much over here. It's black and white, very simple and there's no question it doesn't have the appeal of 'Sledgehammer'. It's very moody and serious." (1987)

Digging In The Dirt

"I think this first video in fact has three words which grow out of the ground, there's 'Dig', 'Help' and 'Heal'. In many ways I think that's a good tag for the album as well." (1992)

And What's More...

On Amnesty International

"In a way, meeting these politicians and so on, we're representatives of what ordinary people feel. Regardless of what these leaders think of us as people and regardless of what egos we may have as musicians. I believe they have to pay some attention to us because of that. We don't have an axe to grind like so many of the lobbyists they meet. When I watched Live Aid I had the sense that this was an expression of the will of the people of the world." (1989)

"I've been keeping myself busy for the past year. But now I want to bury myself in the studio and work on my own album. I'm actually withdrawing from new political involvements for a while. I've worked out that in the last two years these campaigns have taken up six solid months, and that's as much as I'm prepared to give at the moment – also, there's a danger of becoming a benefit whore, isn't there?" (1989)

An Englishman Abroad

"It's well known that I went to a public school, come from a middle class background, and was with Genesis. All these things go with the package and help determine the way I'm perceived. In many other places they don't know and they don't care and I actually feel more comfortable in that situation because I'm being judged on what I'm doing, not on others' perceptions of who I am." (1987)

Opposite: The Conspiracy of Hope Tour line up; Sting, Tracy Chapman, Bruce Springsteen, Youssou N'Dour and PG.

"I only know about 20 words of Wolof…" (1987)

"I love the sound of Italian. French I quite like. German is interesting, but it's not as pleasant to listen to as Italian. The extra syllables you get, the o's and a's that end words, give it an extra rhythm." (1987)

"It's a funny thing. In Nicaragua I was meeting Alex Cox. We were saying goodbye to each other in the middle of the ocean. We shook hands with him and I said to him, Englishman abroad, as we were leaving. That's the only time I've thought it. Otherwise I'm more of a tourist than a businessman. I travel round the cities on my bicycle.
   "I find bicycling is the best way to do it, this kind of travelling when I get a chance. Otherwise you tend to get deposited like a piece of baggage from airport to hotel to gig to hotel. If you have a bicycle you can stop where you want, explore a little, look at a map, ask people the way." (1987)

"I think (Italians) know more than we might give them credit for. There's a lot of exposure to American culture here. There's a lot of similarity in language… I think they love their music and take it more seriously than we do." (1987)

"Like many English people before me I've been attracted to Italy and Africa, societies where emotions are expressed more freely and where people just seem comfier in their own skins. One of the pleasures of arriving at Dakar airport is watching people walking round without hunched shoulders and that slightly fearful gait." (1987)

Fame

"The biggest myth about fame is that it fills holes."

"I don't think you can achieve fame in any walk of life without being a groupie for it in some way or another. There's a part of me that always enjoyed all that, and I need to let it out…I don't take it too seriously, though." (1987)

The Press

"At the end of the day, all journalism has a tendency to try to seize on something a little more interesting… the tabloids are more concerned with keeping their readers in a high state of arousal than they are in relating events accurately." (1987)

"One piece of criticism that sticks in my mind is Paul Morley's critique of my teeth." (1992)

"Apparently during the (Real World) Recording Week, there was some poor bastard who spent three days behind a bush by the railway embankment trying to get a picture of Sinéad (O'Connor) and I, for which he had been offered in-between five to ten grand. Not only was she in America for the whole of this time, but it was raining for most of the period as well." (1992)

"Going out and talking a lot is a period that I could happily live with a lot less of. But it goes with the job, and I've always looked upon it that I have the luxury of making music that I want to make and I have to work a little harder to sell it. I don't think that anyone is successful, whether it's Mother Teresa, army commander or a rock'n'roll musician, unless they have a part of their personality which is comfortable with a lot of attention. You know, I've been doing it a long time and I never took it seriously to begin with, so my ego will enjoy the stroking and pampering it gets occasionally, but I wouldn't like to live there permanently." (1992)

Mark Knopfler, Paul Simon, PG and Eric Clapton.

Philosophy

"I think fantasy and reality are always very confused and I think the confusion between fantasy and reality is one of the things that interests me most. I mean it's like going east and west with fantasy and reality, to either pole, and if you go far enough in one direction you come to the other. If you go far enough into reality you go into fantasy, and vice versa."

"I know I can look into people if I want to now. It's something that happens if you start allowing yourself to be looked into. You get what you give. I used to do some sort of eye meditation. A Japanese meditation which you do with a mirror, where you look at your own image until it disappears. You try and put your consciousness into the mirror image, rather than where you are. What happened for me was that I would get a flash, I would lose myself effectively."

"I am not afraid of failure. There is more to learn from failure than success." (1992)

"The best advice I have ever received is 'In every opportunity, danger; in every danger, opportunity' and 'The last thing man will let go of is his suffering'." (1992)

"Most of all, I love being around ideas, and generating ideas. We have what we call a dinner club, a sort of loose meeting of minds over a meal and several bottles of wine, usually, and we dream. Brian Eno and I have been involved in it for a couple of years, and it's wonderful, it's like a bath for the imagination. We've had lots of different people, architects to technologists to film makers to painters – it's a real blast." (1992)

Religion

"Hymns were a big musical influence on me but only at school. In church I always felt that they were played too slow. I also hated the ritual of church-going."

"I do believe in God. When I think about God, I'm a Buddhist; in moments of fear and despair, I'm a Christian." (1992)

"The music that I would like played at my funeral is 'The Birdy Song'." (1992)

"I would most like to meet The Big One." (1992)

Therapy

"The session I didn't enjoy was the 7.40 am one which meant getting up at 5.30. Which was hard if you'd been working until one or two the night before." (1993)

"There's a line of Kenneth Tynan's…'We find the teeth to match our wounds'. That's very good, I think, the fear that a typically English male has of rooting round in my emotions… it's a dangerous idea, but it's all been enormously useful." (1993)

"It shouldn't be something that we sweep under the carpet. We have to talk about it. Including in interviews. I've been doing therapy of one sort and another for a couple of years now, at first in a couples group and now on my own in another group. I find it enormously valuable. It's like car maintenance, send yourself in to be serviced every few thousand miles and, with any luck, it stops major problems developing. It's much better than waiting for a smash and then trying to put the pieces together."

"I've lived a lot and I've been growing a lot in these last few years. I'm a different person now. So I'm pretty confident in terms of music and not… good in terms of relationships, that's a work area." (1989)

"I have the typical English reaction towards getting help of any sort. Any sort of therapy, baring your soul, admitting sickness, (I have a) natural fear and anxiety about doing anything like that, and yet it's been enormously important to me and really enabled me to get out to the other side, where I still carry a lot of the same stuff, but I'm much better equipped to handle things." (1992)

Marriage and Relationships

"If I consider my current financial situation realistically, I would say that I'd be able to survive in this cottage with my wife and two children living fairly decently for five years… and that's being generous." (1978)

"A lot of the friction towards the end (of Genesis) arose because I wanted to follow up those opportunities and also, I was the first one to have kids. My first child spent three weeks in an incubator, and the doctors didn't think she was going to live.

"Although there was sympathy, it held up recording schedules. The band didn't understand that. For me there was absolutely no question of priorities in a situation like that.

"Now the others have kids they understand. This was one of the factors which helped me think, 'This is not a lifestyle that I wish to continue'."

Peter with ex-wife Jill.

"For a while I used to think it was important to put yourself out there and have an open door approach to your private life, but now I think a little differently. I think that sort of attitude can actually affect the way you live your private life. What you do there and how you do it is very important, so in some ways I'm a little more closed up now." (1987)

"I think I've learnt that there's no such thing as neutral in a relationship. You're either in forward gear or reverse. Forward gear needs work, and no, I don't think there are more forward gears than reverse ones." (1992)

"Well I guess (relationships are) the one part of my life that is more of a struggle than most. I think that many of the things go extremely well for me, sort of work, and that area needs... has room for improvement, let's put it like that. I came out of a broken marriage, and then went into another intense relationship with Rosanna (Arquette), and that broke up as well.
    "So this therapy, which I'd actually started, a couples group, when the marriage went wrong, was something that I did for five years, initially as a couples group, and then afterwards for three years as a single group. That for me was enormously important and that I think made me look at stuff within me that I particularly did not want to acknowledge. There was some anger and aggression in there that I hadn't fully owned up to." (1992)

Family

Above: Peter with Rosanna Arquette
Below: With his daughters Anna and Melanie.

"The characteristics that I think I have inherited from my parents are determination, a love of invention, a love of music and compassion." (1992)

"My most treasured family possession is the videos of my family growing up." (1992)

"I'd like to see if I've still got some friends out there too. The priorities always used to be work, family and friends, with friends often a poor third. The kids still live nearby and I see them every Thursday night and every other weekend... that's what it is. It's hard, very hard for everyone. Messy. But... at least the time I have with them is clear and clean, 'better quality time' as they say in America. That's a real priority, time with my kids..." (1989)

"Parenthood gave me a big sense of who I was, and I worked harder at it than many of my musician friends. Some of the best moments for me have been with my kids. But difficult as it is for their dad, they've got their own lives now. Parenthood is a job that, if you do it well, has planned obsolescence built into it."(1993)

"Having children changes the way you feel about the world. It's like cars, the next model is already there in the market place and will be taking over from you." (1987)

Me

"In my twenties I would have been shocked to think that I would worry about a receding hairline. I thought I was above that. Bullshit! It's still somehow tied up with fears about sexual potency. I get it. Seasonally, I think. I tried treating it with Minoxidil, but it doesn't seem to do much good..." (1989)

"I do feel that sometimes I take too much on my shoulders and don't leave myself enough time to make records. The problem is that I love everything that I do, and I need it because it makes me feel alive and keeps me interested. I need to take risks." (1990)

"At one point I'd planned to do an album project on Death Row, on capital punishment, and I started reading about convicted murderers, what made them tick. I started thinking maybe I was interested in all this stuff because I had something murderous inside me." (1992)

"I hate to be pigeonholed. For me, I don't feel part of the mainstream of what's going on. I'd like to be able to manoeuvre somewhat anonymously in the wings. I think it's unhelpful sometimes when musicians get pigeon-holed as doing one thing or another, 'cause they quite often get lumbered with it for the rest of their life." (1980)

"I think it's true that I tend to hold back my emotions. In a way, I think it's simpler if you do hold back – you can give a calmer vehicle for your message. Ultimately, my passion goes into my music and I'd rather be judged on that." (1987)

"The first thing that I do when I wake up in the morning is switch off the alarm, listen to the stream outside my window and switch on Radio Four." (1992)

"When I'm drunk I'm either miserable or funny, horny and asleep, in no particular order." (1992)

"In a film, I would have Fred Astaire or Groucho Marx to play me." (1992)

"It's partly that I keep myself pretty busy, and it's also that I'm slow and I am a perfectionist. Whereas some people will just get on with it, I'll tend to wait. But I'm well aware that it can go flat." (1993, on gaps between albums)

"I don't like to say no. If I can use my connections, I suppose, to get a few things off the ground, then that's great for me to do, but sticking with them, that is the hard part." (1992)

"Why? Maybe, no and yes are five words to describe me." (1992)

"My problem is that I don't like to say no. I am good at getting things started, at kicking them off, but I'm weak at following through." (1992)

"When I first come up with an idea, nothing can stop me, and then, a while into the process, I'm in neutral gear and I can be uncertain, and that's when I get kicked off course. It's only then that I realise I'm not really in neutral, and just had the clutch down, and when I lift the clutch, I find I'm still going. But, yes, there is that wobble period." (1992)

"Selfishness is my most unpleasant characteristic…I'd say that was at the top of the list." (1992)

"Fear is my greatest fear." (1992)

"Game for a laugh, that's me." (1989)

Ambitions

"I went to a careers guidance thing once. They did all these aptitude tests, and they said there were only two things I was fit for. One was photography, the other was landscape gardening. I think I would enjoy both, actually. Perhaps that's what I do with the music." (1990)

"At one point I thought I had the choice between being a musician and being a farmer – and I am a mixture of both personalities. A more introverted person who loves solitude, nature, ideas. And then there's the other part of me that loves attention, loves being a performer, loves the excitement and cut and thrust of competition in the music business, the whole capitalist circus. So I'm torn between the two, and the only way I can resolve it is by trying to get a good heap of both in my life." (1989)

"The Real World Experience Park is the ambition that I still have to fulfil." (1992)

"If you can make sounds that are interesting, you should continue until you are seventy years old."

What Others Say
About Peter

"For the first few years of working with him, there wasn't a
single person from the road crew that wouldn't have gone out
on a tour for no money at all, just to be involved with this guy
and his calibre of music and professionalism."
(Drummer Jerry Marotta)

"He gets very shy and awkward and makes an awkward face and
mumbles an awful lot. There wasn't a tour, but he thought it best
to let me know he was thinking of trying other musicians. I felt
crestfallen, but then that is natural when you have put over a
decade into it. But it isn't as though it is the only thing that I do.
It's just the way this business works, there are no guarantees. It is
inherent in what Peter does that things are going to change."
(Keyboardist Larry Fast)

"I always think that the way Peter works makes the studio very
much a natural part of his life. If he's not in a great mood then that
sometimes spills over. I think albums three and four are darker, but
that was him not letting his more playful spirits out. I don't know
whether he would agree with that." (Guitarist David Rhodes)

"My attachment to Peter goes back to when I was a teenager.
The first album I ever bought in my life was Genesis's 'Foxtrot'
and the first show I ever saw in my life was Genesis on the
Foxtrot Tour… What has always fascinated me a lot, even before
I got to know him personally, was his strength of character –
because he needed it to dare to quit Genesis at the peak of their
glory… at that moment I really understood that he was
someone special.
    "When I found I was on the same tour as him in Autumn of
1980, I hardly dared to meet him backstage… but today it's
the opposite that happens… he's eaten up by shyness… Beside
Peter Gabriel, Lou Reed and Van Morrison, who for me are the
absolute masters, I will always remain an apprentice."
(Jim Kerr, Simple Minds, 1989)

"What was really touching was that Peter came out on stage and
said, 'I want you to listen to these marvellous musicians, they make
the best music coming out of Africa', which was very humble of
him, he didn't need to do it." (Youssou N'Dour)

"I thought about Peter producing my next record, but Peter said
no, he was not a producer. He said he would sing on it if I wanted
him to, that would make him very happy as he felt very close."
(Youssou N'Dour)

Opposite: With Youssou N'Dour.